Battle Orders • 12

US Special Warfare Units in the Pacific Theater 1941–45

Scouts, Raiders, Rangers and Reconnaissance Units

Gordon L Rottman • *Consultant editor Dr Duncan Anderson*
Series editors Marcus Cowper and Nikolai Bogdanovic

First published in 2005 by Osprey Publishing
Midland House, West Way, Botley, Oxford OX2 0PH, UK
443 Park Avenue South, New York, NY 10016, USA
E-mail: info@ospreypublishing.com

© 2005 Osprey Publishing Ltd.

All rights reserved. Apart from any fair dealing for the purpose of private study, research, criticism or review, as permitted under the Copyright, Designs and Patents Act, 1988, no part of this publication may be reproduced, stored in a retrieval system, or transmitted in any form or by any means, electronic, electrical, chemical, mechanical, optical, photocopying, recording or otherwise, without the prior written permission of the copyright owner. Enquiries should be addressed to the Publishers.

ISBN 1 84176 707 7

Editorial by Ilios Publishing, Oxford, UK (www.iliospublishing.com)
Design: Bounford.com, Royston, UK
Maps by Bounford.com, Royston, UK
Index by Bob Munro
Originated by Grasmere Digital Imaging, Leeds, UK
Printed and bound in China through L-Rex Printing Company Ltd

05 06 07 08 09   10 9 8 7 6 5 4 3 2 1

A CIP catalog record for this book is available from the British Library.

FOR A CATALOGUE OF ALL BOOKS PUBLISHED BY OSPREY PLEASE CONTACT:

NORTH AMERICA
Osprey Direct, 2427 Bond Street, University Park, IL 60466, USA
E-mail: info@ospreydirectusa.com

ALL OTHER REGIONS
Osprey Direct UK, P.O. Box 140, Wellingborough, Northants, NN8 2FA, UK
E-mail: info@ospreydirect.co.uk

www.ospreypublishing.com

Acknowledgements and credits

The author is grateful to Donald W. Boose, Jr. (Col, USA, Ret), Robert Sumner (Alamo Scouts), Leo V. Strausbaugh and Ernie Behnisch (6th Rangers), Russ Blaise (Alamo Scouts Association), David Bingham (Ft Polk Museum), Ben Frank (former Chief Historian, USMC Historical Center), Stewart Kohn, Paul Lemmer, Marine Force Reconnaissance Association, and World War II Ranger Association for their assistance with this book.
Unless otherwise indicated, all the photographic images in this book are from the US National Archives.

Author's note

Marine division and brigade: these are frequently abbreviated to MarDiv and MarBde respectively, following contemporary practice.
Unit designations: Battalions organic to Marine regiments are designated with the battalion and regimental number, for example "1/7" for "1st Battalion, 7th Marines." Companies and batteries are designated in a similar fashion, for example "D/1/2" for "Company D, 1st Battalion, 2d Marines." Army infantry regiments are designated "1/106 Infantry" for "1st Battalion, 106th Infantry."
Unit trees and maps: In the unit tree diagrams and maps in this volume, the units and forces are distinguished by the following colors:

US Marines Corps Raiders and Parachute units:	olive drab
US Army Rangers:	mid-blue
US Army Scouts:	black
Other US Army and Marine Corps infantry:	black
Japanese forces:	red

For a key to the symbols used in this volume, see below.

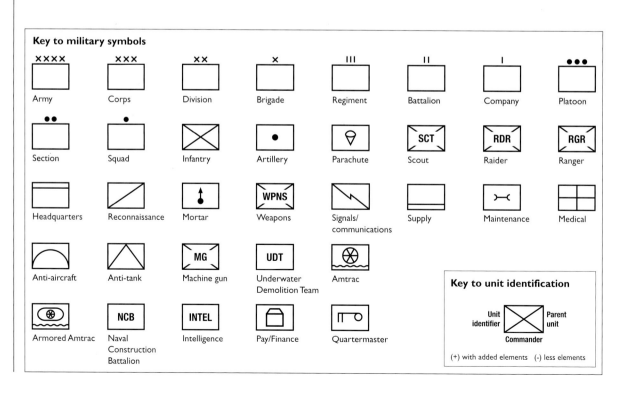

Contents

Introduction — 4
Combat missions

Doctrine and training — 7
Concept of operations • Selection and training

Unit organization — 11
Common organizational practices • Unit designation practices

Tactics — 13
Reconnaissance • Raids

Weapons and equipment — 16
Individual weapons • Crew-served weapons

Command, control, communications, and intelligence — 20
Command and control • Communications • Intelligence

Scout units — 25
The Alaskan Scouts • The Marine Amphibious Reconnaissance Company and Battalion
Amphibious Scouts • 5217th/1st Reconnaissance Battalion • Alamo Scouts

Raider units — 46
USMC Raiders • Provisional Scout Battalion, 7th InfDiv

6th Ranger Battalion — 80
Battalion organization and training • Operations

Lessons learned — 89

Chronology — 90

Bibliography — 92

Abbreviations and linear measurements — 93

Index — 95

Introduction

The Pacific Theater was unique in many ways covering vast distances, remote islands of varied terrain and conditions, weather extremes, a resolute and ingenious enemy, and it required forms of warfare with no precedent. Another aspect of World War II in the Pacific was a serious lack of detailed intelligence information about the islands and the enemy defending them.

This unique environment called for unique units. Six US Marine divisions and 21 Army infantry divisions fought in the Pacific. These were trained and equipped to conduct amphibious operations on rugged islands in a tropical climate. Other specialized units were necessary, ranging from Marine defense battalions, Army and Marine amphibian tractor battalions and amphibian truck companies, Army engineer boat and shore regiments, and naval construction battalions ("Seabees").

A need for still more specialized units became apparent as the Allies thrust across the Pacific. Special amphibious "scout" units were needed to prowl enemy-held islands and collect intelligence. "Raiders", battalion-size amphibious strike units including Marine Raiders and Army Rangers, were needed to keep the enemy off balance and conduct diversions.

No units like these previously existed. They were true pioneers of what is now known as special operations forces. Many of the tactics, techniques, organizational practices, and training methods seen in today's special forces can be traced to these pioneering units.

The men too were special. All were volunteers, met high physical standards, and were selected according to criteria unique to each unit's mission. In some instances they received training within their units, in others they attended special schools. Many of the units are famous and heralded as elite. Others are obscure and virtually unknown. Misconceptions regarding the missions and capacities of some units linger. Some were small, with only a handful of men serving in them. Others were larger with thousands serving. All contributed significantly to the war effort.

All of these units were disbanded during or immediately after the war, their need having passed. Only a couple of units today carry the lineages of any of these units. Most were created, performed their duty, and were never again called to serve.

Half a platoon of Marines re-embark aboard a Eureka landing craft, personnel (large) during joint Army and Marine I Corps (Provisional), Atlantic Fleet landing exercises in July 1941 at New River, NC. Such landing exercises confirmed the need for specialized beach reconnaissance units.

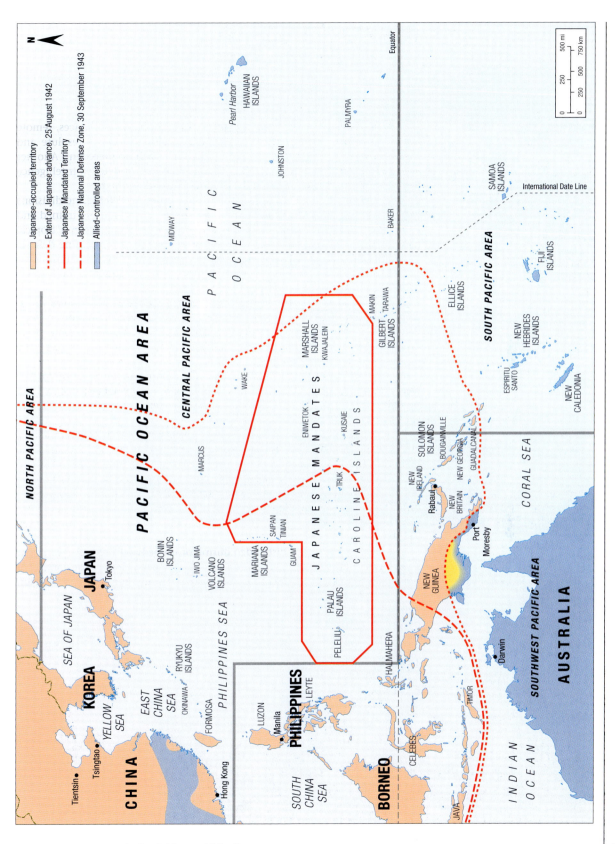

The strategic situation in the Pacific Theater, 1942–45.

Scouts collect and report intelligence information. For the most part they took extensive measures to avoid contact with the enemy or let them know they had been there. Here a radioman transmits information on an Army SCR-300 "walkie-talkie" radio.

Combat missions

While these units may be placed in very general categories of Scouts and Raiders, each had a unique mission or, more accurately, missions, some more specialized than others. Ideally, only Scouts would scout and Raiders would raid—the missions require different mindsets and skills. The expediencies of the Pacific though, the necessity to execute special missions at short notice, and the time required and difficulties of getting the right unit in the right place at the right time because of vast distances and comparatively slow means of transportation meant the mission had to be executed by the special unit closest to the objective. Another reality was that the ever-changing nature of the war saw special units employed somewhat differently than envisioned. It was not uncommon for elements of some of these units to operate together in joint missions.

Scouts had the mission of covertly collecting and reporting battlefield intelligence information. Beach and nearshore water conditions, terrain and vegetation, manmade and natural obstacles, movement routes, enemy dispositions, strength, activities, equipment, defenses, and weapons were their areas of interest. They generally operated in small, lightly armed and equipped teams adept at small boat handling. They avoided contact with the enemy and made every effort to not let him know they had ever been there. They were called upon to sometimes conduct small-scale economy-of-force missions such as securing a small island defended only by an outpost.

Raiders had the mission of executing company and battalion-size raids and harassing attacks using hit-and-run tactics. Raiders struck with complete surprise and extreme violence, usually at night, and withdrew as quickly as they appeared. The goal of such raids may have been to destroy a critical facility, damage enemy morale, collect intelligence information (reconnaissance-in-force), rescue prisoners, or create a diversion in support of a larger operation. These were economy-of-force missions employing a small, well-trained unit to rapidly execute a mission for which a larger conventional unit might require more preparation time. While smaller and more lightly armed than conventional infantry battalions, they were sometimes required to fight as infantry.

Their numbers were comparatively small. Including replacements, about 2,000 men from all armed forces served in the various Scout units. Some 6,000 Marines and sailors served in the Raider battalions and less than 800 in the 6th Ranger Battalion. Over 2 million men from all the US armed forces served in the Pacific Theater.

These were not the only Allied special units to serve in the Pacific Theater: Australian, New Zealander, and Dutch reconnaissance, coastwatcher, and commando units all operated there.

Raiders conducted raids and harassing attacks using hit-and-run tactics. Demolition charges were a basic tool of their trade. Here Marine Gunner (equivalent to a warrant officer) Angus H. Goss, who led the 1st Raiders Demolition Platoon on Tulagi, teaches Raiders how to rig 0.5 lb TNT charges with a time fuse.

Doctrine and training

For the most part, doctrine for these units was what today would be called "emerging doctrine." Essentially, it was made up as they went along. Their tactics and techniques evolved as lessons were learned on operations. There were no manuals, merely general guidance in the form of a stated mission. The commanders and other leaders of these units were truly military pioneers and innovators.

The raid is a doctrinal concept as old as warfare, be it raiding a competing tribe's camp for food, inflicting a crippling surprise attack on an army's encampment, or a group of men crawling across no-man's land to capture a prisoner in a trench raid.

America's first amphibious reconnaissance doctrine was specified by Marine Maj Dion Williams in his *Naval Reconnaissance: Instructions for the Reconnaissance of Bays, Harbors, and Adjacent Country* in 1906: "A marine officer who had had practical experience in topographic work, the construction of semipermanent fortifications and field work and in camping in the field should be assigned to cover that part of the work [adjacent land]." Amphibious reconnaissance was a comparatively new concept in World War II. Granted, beaches had been reconnoitered in some earlier amphibious operations, but it was a rare practice. Getting a ship close into shore to launch longboats at night and in fog, the risk of detection, and the inability to communicate information back to the ship hampered early reconnaissance. The concept of delivering scouts from submarines and flying boats and then going ashore in rubber boats was not examined until the mid-1930s. Nor were sufficiently light and compact radios available until then.

Every man, be he a Scout or Raider, had to be able to swim. This was because of the practice of sea infiltration, and the frequent need to cross rivers, streams, and swamps. Here Marines are taught how to remove their trousers, inflate them, and use them as flotation devices.

Concept of operations

Most of these units operated directly under the control of major commands. The unit planned most of the operation, but it was through the parent command that coordination was effected with other forces and transportation arranged. The parent command provided the unit with intelligence on the target area.

Transportation to the objective area was a major aspect. The distances involved and time factors were key considerations. This required early tasking and detailed coordination with other armed services. Army and Marine air transport units were used to some extent to move special units from their base to staging areas where they would embark on the transportation that would infiltrate them. It was the Navy that delivered and recovered most special units. This was accomplished by flying boat, submarine, high-speed transport (aka destroyer-transport), patrol torpedo boat, and other small craft. Once inserted in the target area the most common means of movement was by foot, but rubber boats, landing craft (detailed from destroyer-transports), and even native canoes were employed. Exfiltration, often more dangerous than infiltration, may have been achieved by the same or a different means. In some cases the special unit linked up with subsequently landing conventional forces.

A misconception many hold regarding the planning and infiltration of small special units is that because of their small size, sometimes just a few men, planning and the difficulties of infiltration are proportionally reduced. This is not the case; it requires virtually the same degree of effort to plan, coordinate, and infiltrate a four-man scout team as it does a company or battalion. The transport resources may have been reduced, but they still required a submarine, destroyer-transport, or flying boat and planning and coordinating for one was little different than for six.

Catalina Flying Boats—PBY
The Consolidated Catalina PBY-series patrol-bombers were introduced in 1936 to become the world's most widely used flying boat. The Catalina name was bestowed by the RAF in 1939 and recognized by the US Navy in 1941. Besides being a torpedo-carrying patrol-bomber, it was extensively used for long-range reconnaissance, search and rescue, anti-shipping night attack, anti-submarine, transport, and the delivery and recovery of Scouts. In the role it would land well offshore on moonless nights to launch or recover Scouts by rubber boat. The early models were strictly seaplanes, but beginning with the PBY-5 in 1940 they were fitted with retractable landing gear to make them amphibians. The two-engine "Dumbo," "Black Cat," "Canso," "P-Boat" PBY-5A (pictured), one of the most widely used models, had a 2,545-mile range and a maximum speed of 179 mph. This long range made the PBY ideal for inserting and recovering covert Scouts in the vast Pacific. Armament was two .30-cal. in the bow, one .30-cal. in the ventral position, and .50-cals in the two waist blisters. It could carry 4,000 lbs of bombs or two torpedoes. It had a 7–9-man crew and could carry up to a dozen passengers or 15,000 lbs of cargo. Catalinas were used by all US armed services, though most employed for covert missions were assigned to Navy patrol squadrons (PATRON or VP), as well as by the British and Commonwealth air forces in the Pacific.

Marines undergo confidence training at the Raider Replacement Training Battalion. Such obstacle courses were routine for any Raider or Scout unit, not only to instill self-confidence, but also agility and endurance.

Special units reported the information they collected or the results of their operation to their parent command. It may have been a small team conducting the mission, but the information they collected could impact on the plans made at high levels and could determine how an entire corps of troops would execute its operation.

Much effort was expended on the means of communicating over long ranges with infiltrated special units. This required rugged, man-portable AM radios using Morse Code communicating with base radio stations in friendly areas. This information was then routed to the higher staff the mission supported. Often though teams did not carry a radio. They reported their information once exfiltrated.

It was originally envisioned that Raiders would conduct hit-and-run attacks to keep the enemy off balance and damage his morale. Reality showed that such small attacks had little impact. Even when successful, the damage they caused failed to reduce enemy capabilities or his overall morale. It often had a negative result such as inducing the enemy to reinforce areas that were targeted for future seizure. When executed as a diversion, they achieved little in forcing the enemy to reposition his troops, although he may have held some in-place rather than allowing them to be deployed to meet the main attack elsewhere.

Some commanders viewed Raiders and even Scouts as shock troops that could inflict severe damage on the enemy disproportionate with their size. This may be true under ideal circumstances, but such units were not to be squandered. They were valuable and expensive assets given the time and effort necessary to train them. The troops that comprised these units were of high quality. Many would have been officers and NCOs in conventional units. Besides the time and effort needed to train special units, if they were wasted on some trivial, but dramatic action, they would be unavailable when needed for truly critical missions.

The argument that special units detract from the resources available to larger conventional units is invalid, so long as special units are employed judiciously and effectively for the critical missions they are intended. If misused, they do drain resources. If used effectively, their value is unquestionable.

Selection and training

First and foremost, all members of these units were volunteers. The specific criteria each unit looked for in volunteers varied, but there were common standards. Excellent physical fitness was essential, not only strength and endurance, but eyesight, hearing, and lack of a past history of serious illness. Physical stamina was essential because of the rough terrain, long duration of operations with spartan rations, and the exceedingly harsh climate. Volunteers

Live-fire training similar to this was common within special units. Realistic training improved self-confidence and prepared men for the sights and sounds of combat.

were required to be able swimmers and have 20/20 vision, no eyeglasses or color-blindness.

Most volunteers were infantrymen (Army and USMC Specification No. 745), but there were seldom restrictions on what military occupation they possessed. Even rear service troops were selected if they possessed the desired attitude and motivation.

Since many of these units operated in small independent elements, it was essential that individuals possess a high-degree of self-confidence, motivation and initiative; good judgment, flexibility, and the ability to work as members of close-knit teams. It was no place for loners. Self-motivation meant they needed to be self-starters; that they could accomplish whatever they were assigned without someone looking over their shoulder. They had to make sound decisions quickly and under stress. Rigid, conventional, by-the-book thinkers had no place in these units. They had to be able to make do with limited resources and be adaptable to rapidly changing situations not addressed in manuals—to think on their feet. Another unique aspect of these units is that in the individual training phase the officers and enlisted men trained together, sharing the same ordeal and experiences. Team members had to have absolute trust in each other.

Finding the volunteers varied depending on the unit's size, location, and time constraints. When time was not an issue, the call for volunteers might be announced service-wide. In other cases, especially when a unit was formed overseas, volunteers were called for from units in the immediate area. In a few instances existing units were converted. The 1st Raider Battalion was organized from an infantry battalion and the 6th Ranger Battalion from a field artillery battalion. Those not desiring to remain in such a unit were transferred and replaced by volunteers. Some units sought men with specific types of experience, especially for Scouts (Specification No. 636).

Volunteers were interviewed to verify their motivation for joining and if they had the necessary abilities and attitude. Many had unrealistic expectations and did not understand what was expected of them. Extensive physical testing was undertaken throughout training. Once selected the first phase of training weeded out the unfit, poorly motivated, and those unable to cope with the pace. This was accomplished through seemingly endless physical training, forced marches, runs, and obstacle courses. Attrition was 40 percent or more. The remaining volunteers underwent gradually more demanding physical training and marches to build them back up. Obstacle courses and training challenges served to build self-confidence. Training usually progressed into small unit tactical exercises,

Teamwork was required to paddle an LCR(L). Here the 10-man craft carries 12 men. They have M1 carbines (waterproofed with plastic and tape) slung across their backs. Rubber life rafts had a rounded bow and stern, whereas LCRs had an upturned, pointed bow for better surf handling.

Boarding landing craft via cargo nets was another important skill. Here ship's longboats are used in lieu of landing craft. A box of supplies is being lowered into a boat from a makeshift debarkation training platform.

Hand-to-hand combat training was another basic skill taught to both Scouts and Raiders—and more extensively than to infantrymen. Here a pup tent pole section is used to take down a sentry in a strangle hold.

patrolling, and land navigation with many being conducted at night on rough terrain. Throughout this, basic skills were taught, similar to what they had learned as infantrymen, but more in-depth: camoflage, individual movement techniques, obstacle-crossing, map and compass reading, hand-to-hand combat, knife and bayonet fighting, field sanitation, jungle survival, and more. Instructors continuously evaluated them. In some units the students assessed each other—peer evaluation, a technique pioneered by the Alamo Scouts. The students' capacity to absorb this rapid-fire training and their ability to work as team members was noted as well. Training progressed into more technical skills: communications, intelligence collection, rubber boats, demolitions, weapons (the latter including all weapons used by the unit as well as Japanese weapons). Tactical exercises were now conducted in the form of the raids and reconnaissance patrols they would be executing operationally. At any time a student could be dropped and returned to his unit.

How this training was conducted varied, some units possessing their own training center located at their base. Others relied on a replacement training unit in the States. Many trained as a unit and qualified their own replacements between operations.

Morse Code radio operator (Specification No. 776) training was a different matter. This skill was essential to most units, and the Army Signal Corps operated several schools across the country for this purpose. In the Low-Speed Radio Operator Course they learned to send and receive 13 words per minute. This was followed by three weeks of field training where they learned to operate and maintain different radios, antenna theory, and how to rig long-wire antennas suspended in trees. The Marines trained their radio operators at Camp Lejeune, NC and Camp Pendleton, CA. Navajo code-talkers were trained at the latter and some served with Marine Raiders.

Unit organization

Special units were often uniquely organized as required by their missions. Others were organized along conventional lines using common terms to identify their echelon, but internally they may have been somewhat different, being of smaller size, having fewer subunits at different echelons, and often possessing specialized subunits not found in conventional units. Their rank structure may have been somewhat different, often with NCOs being a grade higher than found in conventional units. Their staffs were often leaner than those of conventional units of similar size.

Common organizational practices

Most special units were designated regiments, battalions, or companies in the usual military hierarchy. Such titles can be misleading though. While their internal structure may have been echeloned into battalions, companies, platoons, and squads, internally they were very different. They were often smaller in strength than infantry units of the same echelon. Frequently the subunits were not organized in multiples of three, as is common practice. There may have been only two subunits. For example, a reconnaissance platoon may have had only two squads rather than three and these were smaller in strength than conventional rifle squads. In some instances units possessed more subunits: four or six. Units sometimes possessed unique subunits, the demolition platoon in the weapons company of Marine Raider battalions for example. Company weapons platoons, if they possessed them, were often smaller and armed with fewer and lighter crew-served weapons. Scout units usually operated in small independent elements, which may have been designated squads, teams, patrols, or parties varying in size from 3–20 men. Even if a unit's table of organization and equipment (T/O&E) specified a particular size element, their strength would be tailored for the mission.

Headquarters companies were typically small. They required only the minimal service assets deemed absolutely necessary when committed to an operation. When uncommitted they relied on their base or a higher headquarters for service support. Headquarters companies often had only small communications and supply subunits as well as some medical support.

Most special units were compact and agile. This made it easier to transport them into and out of the area of operations since all available transport assets (submarines, destroyer-transports, small craft, aircraft) had space and weight limitations. They were small too as higher commanders did not wish to deny too many troops to conventional units, which were in constant need of replacements because of battle casualties, tropical illness, and rotations. There were only so many qualified individuals available. This meant staffs and service personnel often doubled up on duties, having one job in garrison and another when committed to an operation.

Traditional US organizational concepts were apparent in most units, but some, especially the scout units, used unique structures. This is understandable since the units did not operate in the field as an entity, but in small independent elements. Army Ranger

A facsimile reproduction of the Army's Table of Distribution 7-1045, 30 August 1944, Recon Bn Special, which was largely Filipino manned.

battalions were virtually direct copies of British commandos. A "commando," besides identifying an individual, was also a unit of battalion size. A British commando was organized into six 60-man-plus troops (large platoons) of two sections, each of two subsections. The Americans copied this structure in the Rangers with six 60-man-plus companies (much smaller than customary) of two sections, each with two squads rather than subsections. The Marine Raider battalions were also influenced by the commandos, but used four large companies plus a weapons company, each filling a destroyer-transport. To clarify these terms, in the US the "squad" was the smallest maneuver subunit while the term "section" was used in Commonwealth forces. The US used the term "section" for elements of support or weapons platoons. In the latter case they consisted of two or three small squads with each manning a weapon.

Unit designation practices

These units were numbered in their own series and not in conventional unit series. One-of-a-kind units, the various scout units for example, had unique designations. Often, since they were formed as provisional (Prov) (temporary) units by a major command, they had only an informal title such as the Alamo Scouts, Alaskan Scouts, or Amphibious Scouts. Most were later given formalized designations with this often occurring when they received an approved T/O&E. Previously they had been formed using whatever equipment was necessary, it having been requisitioned from resupply stocks of the parent command. They were still commonly known by the original designation.

Companies organic to separate battalions were lettered in sequence (A to as high as F). Battalions within regiments were numbered 1st–4th and the companies within regimental battalions were lettered in sequence through the regiment. Marine Raider battalions were separate units when first organized and their companies were lettered in sequence within each battalion. When consolidated into the 1st Raider Regiment, the companies were relettered in sequence through the regiment. In most special units, platoons organic to companies were numbered only within the company (1st–3d) and squads were likewise numbered within the platoons only.

A facsimile reproduction of Table of Organization and Equipment No. 7-157S, 2 December 1943. Combat Intelligence Platoon, Alaskan Department.

Tactics

Tactics and techniques varied greatly between units and were highly situational dependent. The ability of these units to adapt to different tactical situations, terrain, and missions was one of their strengths. Flexibility was critical.

Regardless of different situations and terrain, there were similarities between small-unit tactics, patrolling techniques, and the execution of raids. They developed standard operating procedures to deal with "routine" mission tactics and techniques. A major portion of these units' training and qualification courses focused on these actions.

Reconnaissance

Three to 12-man teams usually undertook reconnaissance missions. Sometimes specialists accompanied these teams—guides, engineers, weathermen, etc. One to three days might be spent on mission preparation: means of infiltration and exfiltration, map and sometimes aerial reconnaissance of the objective area, route planning once ashore, coordination of support, communications plans, recognition signals, assembly and checking of equipment and supplies, test-firing of weapons, orienting attached personnel, rehearsals, briefing the plan, and more. Because of the urgency of some missions, only a brief amount of time may have been permitted for preparation.

The team could be delivered to the area of operations by destroyer (DD), destroyer-transport (APD), or a flying boat landing well offshore. Other light craft were used for infiltration, including patrol torpedo boats (PT) and submarine chasers (SC). The team then paddled ashore using rubber boats (LCR). This was a major weakness in reconnaissance operations, not so much because of the possibility of detection, but surf conditions, unexpected currents and tides, high winds, and navigational errors. Moonless or overcast nights were of course preferred, but they heightened the chance of navigational errors by the delivery craft (landing in the wrong place) and they greatly increase the difficulty of cross-country movement in dense vegetation and rugged terrain, and collecting intelligence. Japanese security at their installations and bivouacs was typically sufficient, but their beach surveillance and local security patrols, especially at night, were weak.

Infiltration and exfiltration by rubber boat was the most common means of getting on and off islands. Here, after paddling through the surf, Marine Raiders rush ashore from their beached LCR(L) to begin a long-distance run—all part of their physical fitness training.

Scout teams were delivered to their area of operations by flying boat, submarine, and various small craft. One of the most common small craft was the patrol torpedo boat (PT); capable of high speeds and well armed, they could quickly get a team into and out of an area. They were often camoflaged with shades of green so that they could hide from aircraft under shoreline vegetation, and additional weapons were often mounted. The pictured PT-495 frequently supported Alamo Scout missions. (Alamo Scout Association)

Small landing craft such as the landing craft, personnel (ramp) (LCP[R]) and landing craft, vehicle personnel (LCVP) were used to deliver teams in areas with islands in close proximity to each other, especially in the Solomons. Once a team was inserted in an area rubber boats, landing craft, and native canoes might be used for movement along the coast or on rivers when long-distance movement was required. This was much faster, even though usually conducted at night, than overland foot movement.

The focus of most reconnaissance missions was nearshore water (surf, currents) and bottom conditions, manmade and natural underwater and beach obstacles, beach conditions (sand samples collected, could it support vehicles?), and beach defenses. A deficiency in the planning of many missions, usually on the part of higher headquarters, was a lack of emphasis on collecting information on inland terrain conditions. Assault units were provided with sufficient beach data, but little information on what lay behind. They were often surprised by swamps and the density of vegetation, had little knowledge of the location and capabilities of coastal roads and trails, and were unaware of hills and ridges masked by jungle.

In all fairness to the scouts, they were seldom tasked to collect this information nor permitted the considerable time required. Extreme difficulties with navigation and movement in the dense vegetation and rugged ground at night coupled with increased risk of detection further inland often prevented this. While the high risk of death or capture (which almost certainly resulted in death because of Japanese policy toward captured "commandos") was accepted, little would be achieved if they failed to return with the information they were able to collect.

Information was recorded in notebooks, sketch maps rendered, and photographs taken. If the mission was of long duration information might be radioed back to base. The weight, fragility, and touchy reliability of period radios often ruled out this option. Sometimes information was radioed to a ship or submarine offshore using an SCR-511 or 300. A submarine could receive these transmissions, but could not relay by voice unless a similar radio had been left on board. In order to receive transmissions, the sub had to be surfaced near to shore because of the short range.

Exfiltration and link-up with the recovery craft was more difficult than delivery. The team had to be in the right place at the right time, as did the recovery craft. Recognition signals were exchanged at a designated time. Surf, current, and tide had a major impact on the success of launching rubber boats and getting them into open water for pick-up. Exfiltration required more time and effort than infiltration and required the recovery craft to remain exposed for longer periods of time.

The team welcomed hot chow, dry clothes, and medical attention once aboard. Information of immediate value might be radioed to base from the recovery craft. The team would then work on its report. Once fully debriefed at base, the team would rest, train, and prepare for the next mission.

Raids

A raid is essentially a surprise attack executed on a target located in enemy controlled territory. The success of a raid is dependent upon intelligence available on the target (enemy strength, weapon dispositions, terrain, approach route, etc.), complete surprise, overwhelming firepower, detailed planning and rehearsals, and a high degree of coordination between participating elements.

No two raids were organized or executed alike as there were so many variables. The organization and tasks of the raid force could be quite complex. Raid forces were usually organized into three elements. The assault force conducted the attack by fire and maneuver and might be organized into teams tasked with demolitions, securing prisoners, collecting documentation, and destroying specific equipment and facilities. The support force used machine guns, bazookas, and mortar fire to neutralize the target, suppress adjacent enemy positions, and cover the assault force's withdrawal. The security force deployed elements on routes on which enemy reinforcements might approach and to block the escape of enemy survivors.

Once the raid's objective was accomplished the force withdrew to a rally point covered by the support and security forces. Once all personnel were accounted for and the wounded treated, the Raiders withdrew from the area.

The Marines have a long history of conducting battalion-size raids and economy-of-force actions. This tradition was continued through World War II. While rubber boats saw some use in World War II operations, in most instances the raiding force was delivered by conventional landing craft from destroyer-transports. In only one instance, Makin, were the Raiders delivered by submarines and then went ashore and were recovered using rubber boats. Rubber boats were also used by the Raiders to travel from Segi Point to Regi Plantation after they were delivered to New Georgia by landing craft.

These raids and landings may have been intended to harass the enemy, create a diversion, conduct a reconnaissance-in-force, secure a landing beach for an Army follow-on force, or, more commonly, a combination of these tasks. After accomplishing their mission the Raiders might be withdrawn, relieved by follow-on forces, or given an additional mission. Between 1942 and 1943 Marine Raiders participated in eight amphibious raids in the South and Southwest Pacific. Elements of the 6th Ranger Battalion executed five small-scale raids in the Philippines. The Marine Amphibious Reconnaissance Company/Battalion conducted numerous reconnaissance missions, but also executed six small-scale offensive landings to secure small islands.

Weapons and equipment

Scouts and Raiders required light, compact weapons. Both types of units, for different reasons, required weapons with high rates of fire. Scouts operated in small teams and needed the firepower to break contact with a larger enemy force if discovered. Raiders needed to inflict a great deal of damage in a short time.

Light crew-served weapons were often found at a lower echelon than usual. For the most part these units used the same weapons as conventional units, with a high preponderance of automatics and light crew-served. There were few special-purpose or exotic weapons in use at the time.

Individual weapons

The semi-automatic .30-cal. M1 Garand rifle and the M1 carbine were the two most widely used weapons. The M1 rifle with its eight-round capacity gave individuals a distinct advantage over an enemy armed with a five-round, bolt-action rifle. The M1 carbine had the advantage of being light and compact with a 15-round magazine. Designed for close-range self-defense, it fired a short, pistol-like cartridge, entirely different from that used in rifles and machine guns. However, it was found to lack the range, brush penetration, and knockdown of the M1 rifle. It sounded like a 6.5mm Japanese rifle—which could be advantageous to recon teams behind enemy lines. (The semi- and full-automatic M2 carbine with its 30-round magazine was adopted in September 1944, but was not issued until after the war.)

M7 and M8 grenade launchers were available for M1 rifles and M1 carbines, respectively, in late 1943. M1 grenade launchers were used on M1903 rifles and even after M1 rifles had replaced them, squads retained a Springfield and its grenade launcher until launchers became available for the M1. Rifle grenades included: M9A1 AT, M17 fragmentation, M19 white phosphorus, colored smoke, and colored parachute and star cluster flares for signaling.

Submachine guns were more widely issued than in conventional units for their firepower. Special units not authorized them often had some. All fired the same .45-cal. cartridge as the M1911A1 pistol. They had the disadvantage of comparatively poor penetration through dense brush and bamboo, were relatively heavy, and the Thompsons sounded like a Japanese 6.5mm LMG. The M1928A1, M1, and M1A1 Thompsons were widely issued. The M1 models were a bit lighter, of simpler construction, and lower cost than the M1928A1. With most Thompson production going to the Army and the British, in 1942 the Marines adopted substitutes: the .45-cal. Reising M50 (solid stock) and M55 (folding wire stock). Reising guns proved prone to jamming, especially in sand, as well as rusting. This was not so much because of the design, but because low-quality metals were used and they were made with looser tolerances to speed production. Marines claimed the "Rusting gun" made a poor club let alone a reliable firearm. In late 1943 they were withdrawn. In late 1943 the .45-cal. M3 SMG, or "grease gun," began replacing Thompsons. It was a bit lighter, more compact, and cost less to produce.

The bipod-mounted, 20-round magazine-fed .30-cal. M1918A2 Browning automatic rifle (BAR) served as a squad automatic weapon in many units. The M1918A2 was capable of full-automatic fire only in low and high rates. The bipod and flash suppressor were often removed to reduce its weight and length. Marine

Thompson submachine guns were widely used, but the .45-cal. M3 "grease gun" began to appear more frequently from early-1944. It was intended to replace the Thompson, but this did not occur until after the war. M1 and M1A1 Thompsons supplemented the M1928A1 Thompson, pictured in the weapons sidebar on page 17. The former can be identified by the position of the cocking lever on the weapon's right-hand side, as opposed to on top as per the M1928A1, and the lack of the muzzle compensator.

Special unit weapons 1941–45
.45-cal. M1911, M1911A1 Colt pistols
.30-cal. M1903, M1903A1 Springfield rifles
.30-cal M1903A4 Springfield sniper rifle
.30-cal. M1 Garand rifle
.30-cal. M1, M1A1 carbines
.45-cal. M1928A1, M1, M1A1 Thompson SMGs
.45-cal M3 SMG
.45-cal. M50, M55 Reising SMGs
.30-cal. M1941 Johnson LMG
.30-cal. M1918A2 Browning Automatic Rifle
.30-cal. M1919A4 Browning LMG
.30-cal. M1917A1 Browning HMG
.50-cal. HB-M2 Browning HMG
.55-cal. Mk I Boys AT rifle
M1 grenade launcher (M1903 rifle)
M7 grenade launcher (M1 rifle)
M8 grenade launcher (M1 carbine)
60mm M2 mortar
81mm M1 mortar
2.36in. M1, M1A1, M9, M9A1 AT rocket launchers

A Marine on the Russell Islands sights an M1903A4 Springfield sniper rifle, a modified M1903A3. While mainly employed by the Army, the Marines also used these.

Raiders made some use of the .30-cal. M1941 Johnson LMG with a 20-round side-feed magazine, but it was withdrawn in 1943 and replaced by the BAR.

Marine Raiders also used .30-cal. M1903 and M1903A1 Springfield bolt-action rifles on Guadalcanal and New Georgia until sufficient M1 rifles and M1 carbines were available in late 1943. The Marines used M1903 and M1903A1 sniper rifles fitted with 5x and 8x telescopic sights for an 800yd range. The 6th Ranger Battalion used M1903A4 sniper rifles with a 2.5x sight.

Unit	M1 rifle	M1 carbine	Thompson SMG[1]	Reising SMG	M1941 rifle	M1941 LMG	M1918A2 BAR	M1919A4 LMG	M2 mortar	2.36in. bazooka[2]
Alaskan Scouts	x	x[3]	x							
Amphibious Scouts	x	x	x							
Alamo Scouts	x	x	x				x			
Amph Recon Co/Bn	x	x	x				x	x[4]	x	x
Prov Scout Bn	x							x	x	
5217th/1st Recon Bn	x	x	x							
Marine Raider Bn	x	x	x	x	x	x	x	x	x	x
6th Ranger Bn	x	x	x				x	x	x	x

Notes:
1. M1928A1, M1, and M1A1 Thompsons. M3 SMGs may have been substituted after 1943.
2. M1, M1A1, M9, and M9A1 bazookas used depending on the period.
3. M1A1 with folding stock.
4. Later used M1917A1 Browning HMGs.

Troops of the 2d Raiders pose beside palm-log pillboxes they have destroyed behind Beach GREEN 2 on Cape Torokina, Bougainville. While M1 rifles and carbines were widely issued at this point, the Springfield is still evident. The Springfield-armed man sitting in the foreground has rifle grenade containers strapped to his suspenders.

Hand grenades included the Mk IIA1 "pineapple" fragmentation, Mk IIIA1/A2 concussion, AN-M14 thermite incendiary, M15 white phosphorus, AN-M8 white smoke, and M16 and M18 colored smoke used for signaling.

With a high probability of close combat, these men carried knives such as the M1981 Mk I (integral brass knuckles) and M3 trench, KA-Bar utility, Collins No. 18 ("Gung-Ho"), Fairbrain Commando, and various hunting knives.

Regardless of what equipment tables specified for any of these units, what weapons were actually carried varied. They had the flexibility to tailor the types of weapons taken on any given mission.

Crew-served weapons

Basically Scout units used only rifles, carbines, and SMGs. The Marine Amphibious Reconnaissance Battalion was an exception as it was occasionally given secondary offensive missions. Like the Rangers and Raiders it used BARs, machine guns, and 60mm mortars. The Army's Provisional Scout Battalion was actually a strike unit and used these weapons as well.

The most commonly used crew-served weapon was the .30-cal. M1919A4 Browning LMG. This was an air-cooled 31-lb weapon mounted on a 14-lb tripod. Some use was made late in the war of the M1919A6 with a bipod, metal shoulder stock, and carrying handle and could be mounted on a tripod. The .30-cal. M1917A1 Browning HMG was used by the Marine Amphibious Reconnaissance Battalion. This was a watercooled gun on a heavy tripod. Its employment by this unit was unusual because of its 93 lbs with tripod and water. It maintained a high, sustained rate of long-range fire, which probably explains the logic behind its use.

For immediate light fire support, Raider units employed the 60mm M2 mortar. It could be broken down into three portable sections to allow its crew to keep pace with other Raiders in rough terrain. A few well-placed rounds could make a real difference to the outcome of a firefight.

The 60mm M2 mortar served at company and battalion levels to provide immediate fire support with high explosive and WP smoke. The complete mortar weighed 42 lbs making it as portable as a light machine gun and able to keep pace with the troops it supported. While it had a range of almost 2,000yds, its real value was that it had a minimum range of 50yds, allowing it

The M9 and M9A1 bazookas were introduced in 1944, and were used in addition to the M1 and M1A1 bazookas. The former comprised two-piece tubes, allowing them to be broken down into two sections for easy transport. The difference between the M9 and M9A1 was the latch connecting the tube sections. Both weighed 15.87 lbs and had a 300yd range. They were 61in. long assembled, and 31.5in. in transport mode.

to provide close defensive fire. It was also valuable for providing illumination flares to hamper night infiltration, but these were not available until late 1943.

The 2.36in. anti-tank rocket launcher, or "bazooka," provided infantrymen, for the first time, with a lightweight, man-portable weapon capable of defeating tanks. Capable of knocking out any Japanese tank, it also proved effective against pillboxes and fortified buildings. Four models were fielded during the war. Regardless of which model a unit's T/O&E prescribed, it might have had a later model. The M1, identifiable by two handgrips, saw limited use from 1943. The slightly improved M1A1, with one handgrip, saw wider use and was fielded in late 1943. Both weighed 13.2 lbs, were 54.5in. in length, and had a 250yd range. The much-improved M9 and M9A1 were fielded in mid-1944.

The Raider battalions used British-designed, Canadian-made .55-cal. Mk 1 Boys anti-tank rifles, a carryover from the British Commando organization. Weighing 36 lbs and measuring 72in. in length, it was none too portable in the jungle, especially since it could not be broken down into smaller loads, resulting in its nickname of "elephant gun." While there was little tank threat, the Raiders used them against pillboxes and downed a Kawanishi H8K2 "Emily" flying boat and a floatplane with AT rifles and machine guns at Makin.

Rubber Boats—LCR
Rubber boats were an essential tool for Scouts and Raiders. Whether delivered to the island objective by destroyer-transport, submarine, or seaplane, the boats were the only way to get to and from shore. While Evinrude and Johnson outboard motors were available, they proved temperamental, unreliable, and made too much noise for covert operations, although surf often drowned out their noise. Paddles were the main power source. Several models of landing craft, rubber (LCR) were employed. The most common was the LCR(L) (Large) carrying 10 men. It was 14ft 8in. long with a beam of 7ft 9in. Early models were 16ft in length with an 8ft beam. The seven-man LCR(S) (Small) was 12ft long with a beam of 5ft 11in. A 9.5hp motor was used on the LCR(L) and a 6hp on the LCR(S), giving both boats a speed of 3.5–4.5 knots. Some use was made of the Navy two-man Mk 2 and four-man Mk 4 life rafts. The LCRs were black synthetic rubber, but life rafts were yellow. Even with starlight illumination they shone brightly at night and were usually painted with blue-gray rubber paint. The smaller boats ensured wider dispersion of the landing force, but this made it more difficult to assemble ashore, and they were more easily capsized in heavy surf. The smaller ones were easier to launch from submarines and flying boats.

Command, control, communications, and intelligence

LtCol Fred Beans, CO, 3d Raiders, briefs MajGen Allen Turnage, Commanding General, 3d MarDiv (with map), on the mop up of Torokina Island off Cape Torokina, Bougainville, November 1, 1943.

LtCol Merritt A. "Red Mike" Edson commanded the 1st Raider Battalion from its inception as the 1st Separate Battalion in January 1942 until he was given command of the 5th Marines on Guadalcanal in September 1942.

Command and control

Most of these units operated directly under the command of corps, field army, or theater-level commands. Their mission assignments were made by their parent command. In some instances elements of a special unit may have been attached to support a lower-echelon unit, but they were still under the control of their parent command.

They were tasked with a mission, which the unit itself planned, but the staff of the parent command was involved with coordinating the mission with other forces, arranging for the unit's, or its detailed elements', transportation to and from the objective plus logistics and administration. Fire support may have been required in the form of air strikes and naval gunfire. Gathering available intelligence on the target area, enemy, terrain, weather, etc., was also a major function of the parent staff.

Most of these units had comparatively small staffs and staff officers were often of more junior rank than that held by similar officers in conventional units. Pre-mission planning included the direct involvement of small-unit leaders. This included the reconnaissance team leaders tasked with the mission. Raider battalions, once committed to a short-duration mission were concerned with its execution and little staff coordination and planning was required.

Scout units were seldom committed as units. Small subunits (squads, teams, parties) were infiltrated to conduct individual missions while the rear echelon remained in base. At any one time any number of teams might be committed on missions, being infiltrated and exfiltrated from widely separated areas at different times.

Communications

Radio communications is a key tool of battlefield command and control, but even more importantly for reconnaissance units it enabled them to report intelligence information in a timely manner. While much of this information would later be used in planning future operations and was not time critical, it ensured the success of the mission by allowing Scouts to report the information as they collected it. If they were later neutralized by the enemy the information was not lost.

Radios of the period were often heavy, bulky, complex, temperamental, and not always reliable. Scout teams needed a lightweight, reliable, waterproof radio. What they had was not always ideal. Voice radios may have been used for intra-unit communications, especially by the Raiders operating in larger elements. They were also used to communicate with delivery and recovery aircraft and watercraft. Often the delivery sub or transport would radar track a landing party's rubber boats as they headed for shore and radio course corrections using an SCR-300 or 511 left aboard. Long-range communications with a distant base or shipboard station was the main interest of Scouts. This required an AM radio using Morse Code; voice radio simply did not have the necessary range and

The SCR-300 "walkie-talkie" backpacked radio was used by both the Army and the Marines for voice communication between units, and to coordinate movements with delivery and recovery craft. (William Howard, Technical Intelligence Museum)

reliability. This required a great deal of skill on the operator's part, not just in operating the radio and Morse Code, but understanding antenna theory, selection of different types of antenna depending on conditions, radio wave propagation, and radio field repair.

The following radios were among the most common Army radios used by the other types of units as well. CW means "continuous wave" which means Morse Code could be transmitted on the radio. The range given for radios capable of CW and voice is for voice. The CW range was hundreds of miles depending on the antenna configuration and atmospheric conditions. All of these radios were AM, with the exception of the SCR-300, which was FM.

The SCR-193 was a 234 lb ground or vehicle-mounted base station capable of CW/voice with a 20–60 mile range. The SCR-284 was a CW/voice base station that could be man-packed in three loads including a hand-powered generator. The 110 lb set had a voice range of 15 miles. The SCR-300 was a 35 lb backpack capable of voice only with a 3–5-mile range. The SCR-511 was used at platoon-level, but was also used by recon squads and teams. Known as the "pogo-stick," it was voice only with a 5-mile range. The 20 lb radio was carried slung over the shoulder, and was sometimes used to communicate with offshore subs and ships. The SCR-536 "handie-talkie" was used at platoon-level for communications between platoon and the company command post. The voice handheld radio weighed 5 lbs and had a one-mile range. The SCR-694 weighed 70 lbs and could be jeep or ground-mounted as a base station. Designed to replace the SCR-284, it was CW/voice capable with a 100-mile range.

Marine unit T/Os did not specify numbers and types of radios. They used what was available at the time. This was probably more practical as new radio models were constantly being fielded. The Marines used both Navy and Army models, although Army models came into wider use by late-1943 as the Army was more interested in developing lightweight, man-portable radios than the Navy. These included the SCR-284, 300, 511, and 536.

An examination of the radios assigned to the Alaskan Scouts and Ranger units provides an example of radio allocations.

The Marine/Navy equivalent to the SCR-300 was the TBY-1 and -2 ultra-portable radio, a 37 lb backpacked model capable of CW/voice on line-of-sight. It was not as rugged or waterproof as the "300" though. These

The SCR-511 "pogo-stick" radio was another small-unit voice radio used by Scouts and Raiders. It consisted of two components: the transceiver, with a support pole and a 4ft antenna (not pictured), and a chest pack (shown here) with the speaker to which the earphones were attached (not pictured). (William Howard, Technical Intelligence Museum)

Alaskan Scouts	1 x SCR-193
	3 x SCR-284
	9 x SCR-511
	6 x SCR-536
6th Ranger Battalion	10 x SCR-300
	18 x SCR-536
	2 x SCR-694

were used at company and battalion level. For longer-range communications the TBX-1 to -6 portable radios were available and were similar in capabilities to the SCR-284. These were man-portable, but they could not be operated on the march. It required three men to man-pack the 29 lb transmitter-receiver, 31 lb accessory box with receiver batteries, 22 lb hand-cranked generator for transmitter power, and wire antenna. The TBX was CW/voice capable, and required at least 15 minutes to set up, transmit a message, and break down. A major complaint about the TBX was that it was inadequately waterproofed.

An effective means of ship-to-shore communication was by blinker light using Morse Code, sometimes with infrared filters. Timing had to be right and the sub or ship relatively close to shore. It was somewhat time-consuming and the night had to be fogless, further exposing the sub or ship. Semaphore flags and colored marker panels were used for daylight signaling as well, but only limited information could be conveyed by these means.

Intelligence

Because these units' operations behind enemy lines required precise timing, and were executed against superior enemy forces, they needed more detailed intelligence on their objective than conventional units in order to achieve success. Often sufficiently detailed intelligence was simply not available. The often-scanty information available on objective areas was most commonly acquired from aerial photographs and periscope photographs taken from submarines cruising along the coasts. Even this latter source was not always available to Scout units as the photos were taken by the submarines that were delivering the Scouts on their reconnaissance missions. In order to collect some information on remote areas, higher commands consulted old navigation charts (often no more recent than the late 1800s), seamen's guide books, and former inhabitants of the islands (colonial government officials,

One means of collecting intelligence information was long-range surveillance. The 6x30 M13 binoculars (in the leather case on the scout-observer's left hip) and the 20x M49 spotting telescope were two basic tools for gathering this information.

planters, traders, missionaries, etc.). Even tourists' old photos and postcards were collected. On occasion the services of native guides were employed.

Before discussing intelligence further, the designation of intelligence staff officers and sections must be examined. "2" identified intelligence officers and sections. In the Army battalion, group, regiment, and brigade, intelligence officers and sections were designated S-2. At division, corps, and army-level they were designated G-2 for general staff. The Marines preceded staff numeric designations by a different letter identifying the echelon: Bn—Battalion, R—Regiment, B—Brigade, D—Division, A—Corps Artillery, C—Amphibious Corps, and F—FMFPac. This changed in March 1945 when it was directed that the simplified Army staff designation system be adopted to provide a standard system.

Like much else in the Pacific Theater, intelligence collection was a joint effort. At the beginning of the war the Navy was virtually the sole service with an intelligence organization in the Pacific. The 14th Naval District's Combat Intelligence Unit (CIU) at Pearl Harbor dealt with Pacific Fleet intelligence. The CIU was soon overextended and on July 19, 1942 Intelligence Center/Pacific Ocean Area (ICPOA) was formed from the CIU. While other services were represented on ICPOA's staff, it was still primarily a Navy activity. The expanded intelligence organization analyzed, processed, and disseminated intelligence collected by the different services' many reconnaissance assets. On September 7, 1943 ICPOA was redesignated "Joint" with increased participation by other services. Over 2,000 personnel were assigned to the JICPOA on Oahu and its later Advanced Intelligence Center (AIC) on Guam.

Gen Douglas MacArthur in the Southwest Pacific Area (SWPA) established his own intelligence organization in July 1942 and repeatedly shunned offered OSS assistance, stating he could not afford to wait for the OSS to develop an organization. In reality he desired that all intelligence and special operations activities be under his control and not a separate agency—a wise decision.

When MacArthur established the SWPA on April 18, 1942 he found a disorganized array of US, Australian, British, and Dutch intelligence activities, often duplicating and competing with one another's efforts. He placed all these activities under his General Headquarters (GHQ/SWPA) G-2, Col (later BGen) Charles A. Willoughby, and the Allied Intelligence Bureau (AIB) was established on July 6. The combined organization was subdivided into:

Units relied heavily on natives for intelligence collection, especially in the Solomon Islands and New Guinea. Most were pro-Allied and proved to be loyal and reliable. They reported Japanese dispositions and activities and provided Scouts and Raiders with local knowledge of the islands or area.

Section A	Special Operations Australia
Section B	Secret Intelligence Australia
Section C	Combined Field Intelligence Service
Section D	Far East Liaison Section (aka Military Propaganda)

Section C was responsible for geographic area subsections according to Allied national interests: Philippines (US/Filipino), North-East Area (Australian—Eastern New Guinea, Solomons, Bismarcks), and Netherlands East Indies. This was not entirely to MacArthur's satisfaction, as he had little control over the latter two subsections' activities.

Three other activities under GHQ provided support to the AIB: Allied Geographic Section, Allied Translator and Interpreter Section, and the Central Bureau (cryptographic operations). Operational intelligence collection units supporting these agencies included some of the units discussed in this book plus the Coastwatchers; 1st and 2d Commandos, Fiji Guerrillas; and the Netherlands East Indies Intelligence Service. The Fiji Guerrillas, comprising New Zealander-led Fijians, Tonganese and Solomon Islanders, often supported US forces in the Solomons.

The Islands Coastwatching Service (Operation FERDINAND), originally established in 1919 and reactivated in September 1939, was administered by the Directorate of Intelligence, Royal Australian Navy. As the Japanese rolled through the South Pacific its plans were quickly and often haphazardly, out of necessity, implemented and more coastwatching stations established. The Coastwatchers consisted of native-aided Australian, New Zealander, and British civil servants, missionaries, and planters hiding out on both occupied and unoccupied islands. They were granted RAN Volunteer Reserve officer commissions. The Coastwatchers reported enemy ship movements, aircraft flights, and activities ashore on New Guinea, the Bismarcks, and Solomons via short-wave radio to the Coastwatcher Headquarters in Townsville, Australia. Some US Army and Marine personnel were assigned in 1943 after it was placed under the AIB in July 1942. The Coastwatchers' intelligence reports, which often aided the missions of various special units, recovery of downed airmen and marooned seamen, and small-scale guerrilla activities were invaluable to the war effort.

The AIB was fully operational by October 1942 and Section C's Philippine Subsection, under Capt. Allison Ind, was re-establishing radio communications with American and Filipino guerrillas in the Philippines, from whom signals had ceased in August. Evasion and escape nets were established for escaped prisoners and downed aircrew, and means were developed to disseminate propaganda within the islands. In December the first party was sent to establish direct contact with guerrillas on Negros. Between February and July 1943, five additional parties infiltrated other central and southern Philippine islands. By March 1943 a regular system of supply and personnel infiltration was in-place. In May 1943, the Philippine Subsection was separated from Section C and placed directly under GHQ/SWPA G-2. This story is continued in the 5217th/1st Reconnaissance Battalion section.

Scout units of course were charged with entering areas on which little information was available and collecting it for later Raider or conventional operations. This made their missions that much more dangerous. Raider units too would return intelligence information on the terrain, enemy installations, and activities they encountered on their operations.

Scouts recorded the information they collected in notebooks, made sketch maps, drew diagrams with estimates of dimensions of items and facilities of interest; drew beach profiles and overhead views annotated with water, surf and bottom conditions and obstacles; and annotated maps and made corrections. They also took photographs using 35mm standard Kodak PH-324 and non-standard Leica cameras. Little hand-held tally machines recorded the pace-count to estimate distances walked. For beach and inshore reconnaissance, cords marked at intervals were used to measure distances and depths. Swimmers recorded data on Plexiglas tablets with grease pencils.

Men of the 2d Raiders follow a native guide over a Guadalcanal ridge during the battalion's 30-day "Long Patrol," during which they covered some 150 miles.

Scout units

The Alaskan Scouts

One of the least-known scout units was the Alaskan Scouts. This was because of its low-profile missions, extremely remote area of operations, and a tendency to confuse it with the "Eskimo Scouts."

The fighting in the Aleutian Islands, Alaska, 1942–43.

Formation and training

The Alaska Territorial Guard was established in December 1942 as a volunteer defense unit. It consisted of 6,000 Eskimos organized into three regiments under the governor's control. Many of the platoons and squads were located in far-flung coastal villages and served as coastwatchers. Small numbers of these "Eskimo Scouts" served as guides for Army units.

Prior to the war the Alaskan Defense Command, headquartered at Ft Richardson north of Anchorage, found it necessary to form a specialized unit to reconnoiter and map remote areas of the vast Territory of Alaska. The tortuous terrain, weather extremes, and the demands of simply surviving day to day in the Arctic and sub-Arctic demanded highly experienced men.

BGen Simon B. Buckner, Jr. authorized two longtime Alaskan intelligence officers to form a scout unit in September 1941. Scout Detachment (Prov), Alaskan Defense Command was formed on October 1, 1941 at Ft Richardson with some 60 men. LtCol (later Col) Lawrence V. Castner, Maj William J. Verbeck, and 1stLt Robert Thompson were aided by four experienced NCOs from the two 4th Infantry Regiment companies assigned to Chilkoot Barracks at Skagway. (Castner's father, Joseph C. Castner, had helped organize the Philippine Scouts after the turn of the century.) Castner recruited trappers, hunters, fishermen, prospectors, road engineers, and others with extensive outdoor experience, most of whom were draftees. They also recruited Eskimos, Aluts, and Native Indians from troops in the Regular 4th Infantry and the Alaska National Guard's 1st Battalion, 297th Infantry. Trained topographic draftsmen and radio technicians and operators from the States were handpicked by the unit at the Ft Richardson replacement depot. The experienced Scouts took them on week-long trips into the mountains to teach them survival, hunting, and tracking skills. The specialists passed on their technical skills to the woodsmen with most men learning Morse Code, basic radio maintenance, outboard motor repair, map reading, map plotting, and river navigation. They learned how to make Eskimo animal-hide boats, dog sleds, and snowshoes with training lasting into May 1942. They wore proven commercial and Eskimo cold weather

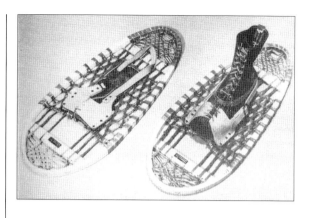

In contrast to other equipment used in the Pacific Theater, the Alaskan Scouts relied on extreme cold weather equipment such as skis, dog sleds, and these "bear paw" snowshoes.

clothing and initially some used civilian hunting rifles. Military discipline was not a matter of concern and neither were haircuts and beards. Rank too was not an issue. When a task was presented, whoever had the necessary expertise took over. They were soon nicknamed "Castner's Cutthroats." Castner though was not the detachment commander, but supervised it with Verbeck in actual command. Castner frequently accompanied it on operations in the Aleutians and assumed nominal command. Capt Robert "Bob" Thompson formally commanded the detachment/platoon from 1943 with a 1stLt Verlakelum second-in-command.

Combat operations

Prior to the American liberation of the western Aleutians, the Scouts were dispatched in small patrols (informally called "groups") and landed in remote areas by seaplanes, PT boats, or sailboats to move on foot or by motorboat to map Alaska's entire coastline. The emphasis was on identifying possible landing beaches and sites for inland airfields that both the Japanese and US might use. After drop-off they would walk or boat down the coastline for hundreds of miles to a village where they would be picked up 30–40 days later. On such expeditions they would carry only staples (flour, salt, sugar) and live off the land by hunting, fishing, and collecting bird eggs. They visited remote Eskimo villages en route and replenished their meager supplies. Besides military weapons, patrols carried .22-cal. rifles for bird and small game hunting.

The Japanese occupied Kiska and Attu Islands in June 1942 as a diversion while the Battle of Midway raged far to the south. Some Scouts focused on the 1,200-mile-long Aleutian Islands chain stretching southwest from Alaska. Others continued to map the mainland coast in critical areas.

The Scouts' first combat operation was to secure Adak Island in the central Aleutians. Castner and 37 Scouts were delivered to the island by the USS *Triton* (SS-201) and *Tuna* (SS-203) on the night of August 28, 1942. They paddled ashore in rubber boats and spent the night scouting the island for a Japanese presence. The all clear was given to overflying aircraft and 2/134 Infantry landed; but they had not been informed the Scouts were present, resulting in some tense moments when contact was made. Six Scouts remained to teach the infantrymen and engineers survival skills and how to live on the barren island. Adak was developed as a naval operating base and airbase for future operations into the western Aleutians.

The Scouts reconnoitered many other islands for signs of Japanese visits and escorted engineers surveying airfield sites and naval installations. In December 1942, while escorting engineers surveying an airfield on Amchitka Island, they discovered the Japanese had recently been there for the same purpose. Scouts again remained on the island to assist the troops building an airfield and endured numerous air attacks from Kiska.

During the May 8, 1943 assault of Attu Island, most of the Scouts were attached to the 7th InfDiv's 17th and 32d Infantry as scouts, guides, and advisors on cold weather operations, effective May 2. One Scout patrol landed between Beaches SCARLET and RED on the north coast for security. Other Scout patrols reconnoitered nearby islands for signs of the enemy as the battle was fought. Scouts accompanying the 32d Infantry went ashore early under Capt. Thompson with the regimental commander and beachmaster. Among the Scouts were Aluts familiar with Attu. They crept toward shore in LCVPs through dense fog, then boarded plastic boats, went in through the offshore rocks, landed, and scouted the beaches. They later guided the assault waves ashore to land unopposed (the Japanese were dug-in on inland hills). During the battle, Scouts often went ahead of the infantry singly and in pairs to select routes through the hills as the Japanese were pushed inland. Attu was secured on May 29 after a brutal fight. One scout was KIA and two WIA.

For the 1943 Kiska Island assault (15 August), half of the Scouts were attached to the 1st Special Service Force (FSSF) directly under Col Castner as the acting commander, even though he was suffering from cancer. The others were held in reserve on Amchitka. The Scouts and FSSF landed on the island's north side while some Scouts landed in Gertrude Cove on the south side as a diversion. The Japanese had evacuated the island, but the Scouts aided in its thorough search.

With the Japanese driven from the Aleutians, the Scouts resumed their mapping of the coast and would map all 34,000 miles of it. In the winter they traveled by dog sled, snowshoe, and cross-country ski. A three-month expedition mapped Nunivak Island north of the Aleutians. Another expedition in the spring of 1944 saw the Scouts building five powerboats and a barge themselves. They were taken by train north from Ft Richardson to map the western Yukon River and Norton Sound on Alaska's west-central coast, a trip lasting into the fall. Another Scout expedition mapped a pipeline route from Fairbanks in central Alaska to the as-yet-to-be-developed Point Barrow oilfields on the north coast.

1943: the 1st Combat Intelligence Platoon

On November 6, 1943 the Scout Detachment (Prov), Alaskan Department (as Alaskan Defense Command was redesignated on November 1, 1943) was redesignated the 1st Combat Intelligence Platoon, Alaskan Department and lost its provisional status.

It was organized under T/O&E 200-2S-A1-6 dated December 2, 1943. This was changed to T/O&E 7-157S on September 29, 1944 with no change in manning. (It is interesting to note that T/O&E 7-157 was assigned to the Army's new long-range reconnaissance patrol (LRRP) companies formed in 1961.) The T/O&E authorized two officers and 86 enlisted. Unfortunately the T/O&E does not provide a breakdown for internal organization. It had a small headquarters with a captain, 1st lieutenant, platoon (technical) sergeant, and a few draftsmen and radio technicians and operators. It was completely lacking in service personnel as it relied on higher command for administration and services.

The T/O&E lists three staff sergeant patrol leaders and seven assistant patrol leaders, but the breakdown of enlisted men by rank and specialty does not provide for a balanced distribution of personnel between an unspecified number of patrols. Tailored patrols were organized from a pool of personnel and assistant patrol leaders often served as patrol leaders. Up to 10 such patrols could be formed, typically consisting of a patrol leader, two or three Scout guides, two or three Scout observers, a topographic draftsman, and a radio operator. Again it is emphasized that patrols were tailored for missions and ranged from 4–12 men. The platoon's armament included M1911A1 pistols, M3 SMGs, M1 rifles, and carbines. Every man was authorized an M3 trench knife, but many carried a favorite hunting knife. Emphasizing their reconnaissance mission, every man was issued a wrist compass and a pair of M13 binoculars.

Alaskan Scouts served as guides for 7th InfDiv units landing on Attu Island; they provided information on the island and local conditions, and acted as cold weather advisors. Here mountain rucksacks, used by the Scouts, are stacked on the Massacre Bay landing beach. In the background a tractor off-loads from an LCM(3).

The shoulder sleeve insignia of the Alaskan Scouts, October 1941–November 1943.

The shoulder sleeve insignia of the Alaskan Scouts, November 1943–December 1945.

The battle blaze of the Amphibious Reconnaissance Battalion, FMFPac, August 1944–September 1945.

The Alaskan Scouts were inactivated at Ft Richardson in December 1945 and most of the personnel were discharged.

The Marine Amphibious Reconnaissance Company and Battalion

In early 1938 the 1st MarBde tested the concept of delivering four-man patrols by submarines off a planned landing beach. The patrols paddled ashore at night using four-man life rafts. The missions, conducted during Fleet Landing Exercise (FLEX) 4 at Vieques and Puerto Rico were of mixed success. Both patrols were captured, but it was realized that with experience and refinement the concept held promise. By FLEX 6 in 1940, patrols were successfully infiltrating ashore and reporting information. Marine units had become reliant on the information and it was now an accepted doctrine.

To provide a dedicated amphibious reconnaissance unit, the 22-man Scout-Observer Group was formed in January 1942 at Marine Barracks, Quantico, VA. Its personnel were largely drawn from 1st MarDiv battalion and regimental intelligence sections. Most came from the 5th Marines along with a small number of personnel from the Army's 1st Div. This experimental unit was assigned to the joint Marine and Army Amphibious Force, Atlantic Fleet. On March 2, it was redesignated Amphibious Corps, Atlantic Fleet. Originally the unit prepared for the invasion of North Africa, but the Marine Corps reoriented toward the Pacific. On August 24, the Amphibious Corps was dissolved and the Marine elements were redesignated Amphibious Training Staff, Fleet Marine Force (FMF).

During this period the Scout-Observer Group experimented with reconnaissance techniques, different types of small boats (rubber, folding canvas, kayaks), outboard motors, radios, signal lights, and other equipment. Training included forced marches, beach runs, reconnaissance techniques, radio operation, land and sea navigation, and swimming.

In December the Marine element of the group moved to Camp Elliot, CA, was assigned to Amphibious Corps, Pacific Fleet, and grew in size with 2dLt Merwin H. Silverthorn, Jr. commanding. The Marine Corps soon assigned 1stLt James L. Jones, a former Army Reservist, to command the group. At 27 he was considered too old for commissioning in the Marines, but his experience as a tractor salesman in North Africa and the fact that he spoke French gained him the assignment.

On January 7, 1943 the Scout-Observer Group was redesignated Amphibious Reconnaissance Company, Amphibious Corps, Pacific Fleet under T/O D-817 dated December 21, 1942 with six officers and 92 enlisted. (Marine divisions possessed a scout company, redesignated reconnaissance in April 1944, employed for tactical reconnaissance, division reserve, HQ security, and to plug frontline gaps.) Armament included M1 rifles, carbines, BARs, and one M1919A4 LMG per platoon. Radios were the SCR-511 and TBX.

The company continued to train, mostly on Camp Pendleton, perfect techniques, and test equipment. During this time it assisted with the training of the 7th InfDiv's Prov Scout Battalion bound for the Aleutians. On August 25, 1943 Amphibious Corps, Pacific Fleet was redesignated V Amphibious Corps (VAC) and the company's designation too was changed. Most commonly they were known simply as the "Recon Boys." In September the company deployed

Amphibious Reconnaissance Company	
Company HQ	2 off. 16 enl.
Reconnaissance Platoon (x4)	1 off. 19 enl.
Platoon HQ	1 off. 7 enl.
Reconnaissance Squad (x2)	6 enl.

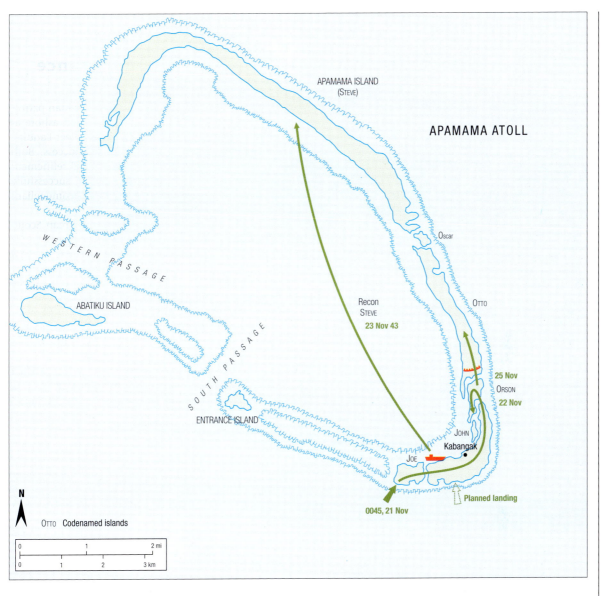

Amphibious Reconnaissance Company, VAC on Apamama Atoll, Gilbert Islands, November 21–25, 1943.

to Camp Catlin, Oahu, Hawaii with VAC. This would be its base after every return to Hawaii. Capt. Jones was detached for duty aboard the USS *Nautilus* (SS-168) during its reconnaissance of the Gilberts in September and October 1943. The company XO, 1stLt Silverthorn, was the acting CO.

Combat operations: Apamama and Makin Atolls

Upon Jones' return the company, less 4th Platoon, embarked aboard the *Nautilus* and departed Pearl Harbor for the Gilberts. A 102d Engineer Combat Battalion 10-man bomb disposal squad was attached along with three liaison/survey officers. The company would reconnoiter Apamama Atoll (BOXCLOTH) on November 20, D-Day on Tarawa 76 miles to the northwest. The 2d MarDiv assaulted Tarawa that day while the 27th InfDiv seized Makin further north. The company's mission was to determine if Apamama was occupied in strength. If occupied by only an outpost it was to overcome it. If a large force was present they would withdraw and the 2d MarDiv's 3/6 Marines would seize the island on the 26th. On the 19th, while cruising surfaced near Tarawa on the lookout for pilots downed when bombing the island, the *Nautilus* was fired on by the USS *Ringgold* (DD-500) and damaged by two 5in. rounds, one a dud. Forced to dive, she made repairs and continued to Apamama.

The northwestern side of the atoll is lined with several low, long, narrow islands densely covered by palms. The 78 Marines and soldiers went in using six LCR(L)s at 0045 hours, November 21 and landed on a south-end islet codenamed JOE. They were supposed to land on JOHN, a larger islet to the east, but the current carried them beyond. Four of the LCR outboard motors failed and they had to paddle ashore, arriving by 0500 hours.

The provisional machine gun section and demolition squad established a perimeter. The three platoons moved north up the island detailing 1st Platoon to keep a beached Japanese barge under surveillance. They encountered two natives known to the Australian liaison officer, reported the location of 23 Japanese, and that they knew the Marines were ashore. The 3d Platoon disabled the barge after encountering three Japanese and killed one. The 1st and 2d Platoons and the machine gun section advanced encountering five Japanese, killing two. In the late afternoon, after crossing the reef to OTTO from ORSON, the Marines came under fire. Being exposed, they withdrew to OTTO. They had been unable to contact the *Nautilus* by radio, but the sub had followed their progress by colored panels the Marines hung in trees. All supplies and equipment were moved from the beachhead to the new position on the morning of the 22d. The small company was unable to advance during the day because of the enemy's ability to cover the 400yd-wide, knee-deep reef separating the islets. In the early evening the *Nautilus* made contact with the Marines and supplies were boated ashore. The 23rd saw a continued stalemate, but the Marines were able to rubber-boat to STEVE Island to the north of Japanese-held OTTO and reconnoiter it for an airfield. Two injured Marines, one of whom later died, were evacuated to the sub. Capt Jones went aboard and coordinated fire support for the next morning's attack. Pre-dawn on the 24th the Marines reoccupied ORSON. At 0810 hours 1st and 2d Platoons assaulted on the right with 3d Platoon and the machine gun section providing covering fire. The *Nautilus* fired 70 rounds of 6-in. on the Japanese with no apparent effect. Many of the Marines were pinned down, unable to withdraw, and suffered one KIA and two WIA. The USS *Gansevoort* (DD-608) arrived on-station and shelled the Japanese position from 1800–1900 hours. In the meantime Jones was heading to sea in the *Nautilus'* whaleboat to contact the transports bearing 3/6 Marines. The ships withdrew when a Japanese submarine was sighted. On the morning of the 25th a native reported the Japanese had lost some men and left their position. Jones feared they might attack the beachhead and seize the whaleboat. While preparing the defense another native arrived reporting the Japanese had committed suicide. The Marines investigated and found 23 bodies. 3/6 Marines arrived on the morning of the 26th; the recon Marines boarded the USS *Harris* (APA-2) and departed. The Marine 8th Defense Battalion garrisoned the atoll and a bomber field was built.

In the meantime the company's 4th Platoon had accompanied 165th Infantry to Makin Atoll. On November 20 it and 2d Platoon, G/2/165 Infantry secured Kotabu Island north of the west end of Butaritari Island, the atoll's main island. The reinforced 165th Infantry landed on Butaritari on the 20th and the 4th Platoon fought with them on November 21–22.

Majuro Atoll, 1944

The company reassembled on Hawaii and prepared for its next mission. Training incorporated the many lessons learned on Apamama. For example. a 23-man mortar platoon with four 60mm mortars was added on January 3. Jones felt that if mortars had been available they could have suppressed the Japanese on OTTO and fought across the intervening reef.

Covert subs

The use of submarines to deliver and recover Scouts and Raiders from objective areas was often preferable to aircraft and surface ships. Flying boats and ships could travel to the area faster, but they were more vulnerable to detection. Once the landing party was delivered the sub could remain in the area using radar to detect incoming aircraft and ships and warn the troops ashore, relay communications, send emergency supplies ashore, provide fire support, receive and treat wounded, and conduct its own photo-reconnaissance of the island's shores. While standard fleet subs were employed to deliver and recover scouts and raiders, three subs had been modified for the role. The USS *Narwhal* (SS-167), *Nautilus* (SS-168), and *Argonaut* (APS-1) were cruiser subs built in the late-1920s. They were 360ft in length, 50ft longer than fleet subs and almost as long as a destroyer, and displaced almost 3,000 tons. They were armed with torpedoes and two 6in. guns. Their operational range was 18,000 nautical miles. The *Argonaut* (formerly SS-166) had been converted to a transport sub in early 1942 and could carry 120 troops. It was sunk in January 1943. The others could carry 90–100. For operations supporting Philippine guerrillas, 19 subs completed 40 missions delivering 331 personnel and 1,325 tons of supplies, and evacuated 472 personnel with the loss of only one sub. They could carry up to 20 passengers and 100 tons of cargo.

Majuro Atoll (SUNDANCE) is in the southeast portion of the Marshalls and north of the Gilberts. The Japanese had a seaplane base on small RITA on the elongated atoll's northeast corner. Majuro would be secured by recon Marines while the 4th MarDiv and 7th InfDiv seized Kwajalein Atoll 280 miles to the northwest in the central Marshalls. It would be used to secure the line of communications with the Gilberts and protect that route from Japanese-occupied atolls to the north and south. The SUNDANCE Landing Force consisted of 2/106 Infantry, 27th InfDiv and Amphibious Reconnaissance Company, VAC. The Marshalls were part of the Japanese Mandated Territory, making the recon Marines who landed on Majuro the first Americans to set foot on Japanese territory held before the war.

The Majuro Attack Group (TG 51.2) departed Hawaii with the company aboard the USS *Kane* (APD-18). It arrived at Majuro on the night of January 30 outside the atoll's north entrance. The 4th Platoon, a mortar section, and company headquarters troops landed on LUELLA, an islet on the east side of the entrance, aboard an overloaded LCP(R). They had abandoned two LCR(L)s because of the inability to tow them in high seas. A native reported up to 400 laborers were on RITA. Sixteen men went to LUCILLE, a tiny islet in the middle of the entrance, and searched it before dawn. In the meantime it was realized that the native had been mistranslated and all but four of the Japanese had departed much earlier. However, the rest of the company was rushed to ROSALIE adjacent to RITA.

The company (-) landed on ROSALIE between 0200–0400 hours on the 31st. A native reported that only a Japanese warrant officer and three civilians were present on LAURA on the atoll's opposite end. The company, including 4th Platoon, re-embarked aboard the *Kane* that evening and headed for LAURA. The 4th Platoon landed on LAURA at 2145 hours. They patrolled the island and captured the warrant officer on February 1; the civilians eluded capture. Another platoon searched Arno Atoll 10 miles to the east on the 1st with no results. The company then sailed for Kwajalein on the 2d. There it was attached to Tactical Group 1, VAC, a provisional Marine force consisting of the 22d Marines and 106th Infantry. The brigade-size force sailed for Eniwetok Atoll (DOWNSIDE) on February 15 aboard the Eniwetok Expeditionary Group (TG 51.11).

Eniwetok
Eniwetok is 337 miles northwest of Kwajalein, and 3,450 Japanese were dug-in on the atoll's three largest islands. On February 17, TG 51.11 arrived and as on Majuro the company secured entrance islands. At 1320 hours 60 men were landed by LVT(2) amphibian tractors on CAMELLIA to the southeast of defended Engebi Island. Another 61 recon Marines landed on CANNA 10 minutes later. Both islands were unoccupied and artillery battalions were emplaced to support the assault. From February 18–21 the company searched the atoll's 29 unoccupied islets. One Marine was KIA and two WIA on ARBUTUS by stray fire from Engebi. On the 23rd the company landed on Parry Island on the atoll's southeast rim, coming ashore in the early afternoon on Beach GREEN 2 on the west shore of the atoll's second largest island. There the 22d Marines were in need of reinforcement as it battled on the most strongly defended of the islands. The company was split into two roughly 55-man groups. Jones and the 1st and 2d Platoons were attached to E/2/22 while 1stLt Silverthorn and the 3d and 4th Platoons supported F/2/22. The Mortar Platoon was split between the two groups. This reinforcement allowed the battalion to clear the island. The company suffered no losses, was released back to Tactical Group 1 control, and re-embarked aboard the *Kane* on the 24th. Transferred to the USS *Neville* (APA-9), the company returned to Hawaii.

The 1944 Amphibious Reconnaissance Battalion
The company had difficulties preparing for its next operations, training replacements, and absorbing the lessons learned. Recovery time between

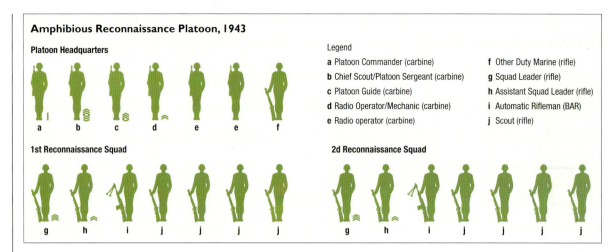

operations was limited. To provide more flexibility the company was expanded into Amphibious Reconnaissance Battalion, VAC on April 28, 1944 under T/O E-335 with 20 officers and 282 enlisted. Jones was promoted to major, Capt Earl Marquardt was XO, Capt Silverthorn commanded Company A, 1stLt Russell Corey took Company B, and 1stLt Leo Shinn the HQ Company.

The battalion staff was extremely lean. The commander was a major, the XO a captain, and all other staff officers were 1st lieutenants. The Bn-1/Adjutant (personnel) doubled as the HQ Company commander. The Bn-3 (operations and training) doubled as the Bn-2. There was also a Bn-4 (supply) and a communication officer/communication platoon commander. The 20-man reconnaissance platoons had a seven-man HQ and two six-man reconnaissance squads each with a BAR. Both M1 rifles and carbines were carried. Though not on the T/O, Thompson SMGs were used. All hands carried KA-Bar knives.

The weapons platoon had an HQ identical to the reconnaissance platoon's. The two weapons squads had the same rank and duty positions as the reconnaissance squads, but with an M1 rifle-armed mortar gunner replacing the BAR-man. The weapons platoon had a pool of weapons to be manned by weapons squad, platoon HQ, and detailed company HQ personnel as required for the mission. The platoon HQ and both squads had an M1917A1 HMG and a 60mm M2 mortar while the squads each additionally had two 2.36in. M1A1 bazookas. Moreover, the weapons platoon could serve as a reconnaissance platoon.

The companies were operational by June 30 and the new HQ Company on July 15. The battalion departed Hawaii for the Marianas aboard the USS *Stringham* (APD-6) and USS *Cambria* (APA-36) in early July with 312 men. On

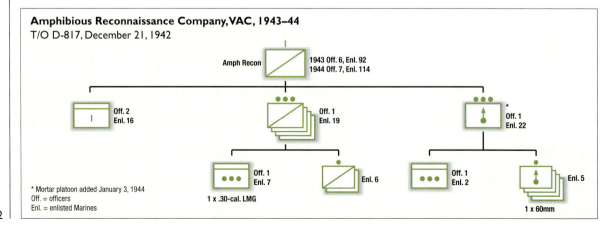

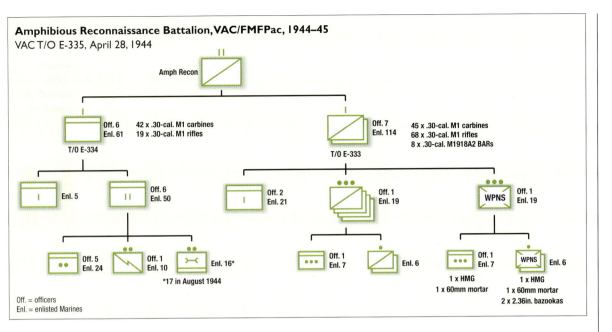

June 14 Company A was to land at Laulau on Saipan's east coast with 1/2 Marines (Eastern Landing Group) to seize inland Mount Tapotchau the night before the main landing. This operation was wisely canceled, as the force would in all probability have been cut off.

Amphibious Reconnaissance Battalion	
HQ Company	6 off. 61 enl.
Battalion HQ	6 off. 50 enl.
HQ Section	5 off. 24 enl. (13 USN)
Communication Section	1 off. 10 enl.
Maintenance & Supply Section	16 enl.
Company HQ	5 enl.
Reconnaissance Company (x2)	7 off. 114 enl.
Company HQ	2 off. 21 enl.
Reconnaissance Platoon (x4)	1 off. 19 enl.
Weapons Platoon	1 off. 19 enl.

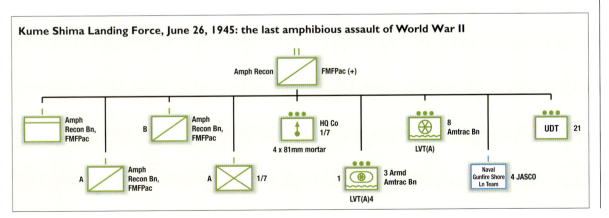

VAC had been fighting on Saipan since June 15 and would continue to July 9. Tinian (TEARAWAY) is a 5 x 10.5 mile island 3 miles south of Saipan. The 2d and 4th MarDivs wrapping up the Saipan operation were assigned the shore-to-shore assault, but the Japanese heavily defended the preferred beaches on Tinian. The Navy favored a direct assault into heavily defended Tinian Harbor on the lower west coast. The Marines were willing to risk an unconventional landing on two extremely narrow beaches (60 and 160yds wide as opposed to the preferred 1,200yds) on the island's northwest end. While Marine and Navy planners argued their cases, teams of recon Marines and swimmers from Underwater Demolition Teams (UDT) 5 and 7 conducted a joint reconnaissance. The recon Marines would reconnoiter the beach and the immediate inland area while the UDT men examined the reef and surf conditions. Rehearsals were conducted at Magicienne Bay on Saipan's southeast end on July 9/10. On the night of July 10/11 a Company A team and UDT men reconnoitered Beach YELLOW at the northeast end. They confirmed that this larger beach was well defended, mined, and extensive obstacles were present. In the meantime a Company B team, now operating from the USS *Gilmer* (APD-11), with UDT counterparts, were to reconnoiter Beach WHITE 2. Strong currents carried them past the objective to WHITE 1 1,000yds northeast. They completed its reconnaissance and returned safely. The next night a Company A team with UDT swimmers successfully reconnoitered WHITE 2. It was confirmed that the narrow beaches were virtually undefended, free of obstacles, and no mines were detected. The decision was made to use these unconventional beaches for the July 24 (J-Day) assault. The battalion remained off Tinian until August 9, and unneeded, it returned to Hawaii on the SS *Azalea City*.

With the activation of Fleet Marine Force, Pacific (FMFPac) on July 12, the battalion was redesignated Amphibious Reconnaissance Battalion, FMFPac on August 26 with no change in organization other than a strength increase of one man.

1945 operations: from Iwo Jima to Kume Shima
Company B accompanied VAC to Iwo Jima (ROCKCRUSHER) in mid-February 1945 aboard the USS *Bladen* (APA-63). Three men accompanied a pre-landing reconnaissance of the east and west beaches with 22 men from the 4th and 5th MarDivs' reconnaissance companies and UDT men on February 17. After the February 19 (D-Day) landing the company's only operation was a reconnaissance-in-force of Kangoku and Kama Rocks 2,250 and 1,000yds northwest of Iwo Jima. On March 13 officers and NCOs of the company boarded LVT(A)4s of the 2d Armored Amphibian Tractor Battalion and scouted the islets without landing to report they appeared unoccupied. The next morning 100 men of the company landed on the islets using LCR(L)s and confirmed they were unoccupied. Fire support was provided by 90mm guns of the Army's 406th Anti-aircraft Artillery Battalion. The company withdrew, boarded LST-784, and was ordered to Okinawa. After transferring to the USS *Chase* (APD-54) at Saipan, it arrived on April 4.

In March the Battalion HQ and Company A were sent to Leyte aboard the USS *Kinzer* (APD-91) and *Scribner* (APD-122) to link up with the 77th InfDiv preparing to seize the Kerama Retto, a group of small hilly islands west of Okinawa (ICEBERG). As the 77th stormed the islands from March 26–29, Company A reconnoitered islets off Okinawa's lower west coast prior to the April 1 (L-Day) landing by Tenth Army (IIIAC and XXIV Corps): Keise Shima on March 26/27 (on which were emplaced two 155mm gun battalions), Aware Shima on March 27/28, and Mae Shima and Kuro Shima on the 29th. No enemy were found. After the arrival of Company B, six islets on the east side of Okinawa were searched from April 6–8. Japanese were discovered only on the first islet, Tsugen Shima. The battalion withdrew and the Army later cleared it. On April 12/13 the battalion landed unopposed on Minna Shima, an islet between northern

Okinawa and Ie Shima 4 miles south of the latter. Three Army artillery battalions were positioned on Minna to support the 77th InfDiv's seizure of Ie Shima. The battalion then searched numerous islets off Motobu Peninsula on Okinawa's upper west coast as the 6th MarDiv secured the peninsula.

The battalion's last action, and the last amphibious assault of World War II, albeit unopposed, was conducted on June 26. Kume Shima, 55 miles west of Okinawa, was secured on June 26–30 to establish an air warning radar site and fighter direction center. Reinforced by other units, the battalion landed on the island's southeast shore meeting no opposition from the estimated 50-man garrison. In early July the Japanese were engaged in two firefights and scattered. For the operation the battalion was reinforced with attachments and was in overall command of the assault.

The battalion departed Okinawa on August 1 and was aboard the USS *Elkhart* (APA-80) at Ulithi Atoll planning its part in the invasion of Japan when the first atomic bomb was dropped. It sailed for Hawaii aboard the SS *President Johnson*, arriving on September 12. Maj Jones was transferred to the States after 25 months in the combat zone. Capt Markovitch commanded until the battalion was deactivated at Camp Catlin on the 24th. Most personnel returned to the States for discharge or reassignment. The battalion had received several written commendations, but only the Navy Unit Commendation as a formal unit award covering all its operations because of its classified nature.

Amphibious Scouts

The Seventh Fleet was assigned to support MacArthur's New Guinea and Philippines campaigns. A key component of the Fleet was the Seventh Amphibious Force, commissioned as Amphibious Force, Southwest Pacific in January 1943 and redesignated in March 1943. This force, although provided with meager assets when compared to the Third and Fifth Amphibious Forces in the Pacific Ocean Area, would conduct more amphibious operations in the Southwest Pacific (New Guinea, Philippines, East Indies) than the other two forces combined in their area. The Army's 2d–4th Engineer Special Brigades supplemented it. (The Army's Engineer Amphibian Command had grown as a result of the Navy's inability to provide sufficient landing craft for projected operations. The EAC's special brigades each had two boat and shore regiments, each with 1,100 landing craft, to conduct shore-to-shore landings. They also provided shore-party services and landing craft maintenance.)

Formation and training

New Guinea's extensive north coast was poorly charted. US and Australian forces would conduct numerous landings on its remote shores and offshore islands. The commander of the Seventh Amphibious Force, RAdm Daniel E. Barbey, established an Amphibious Scout School at Cairns on Australia's northeast coast in April 1943. Two Marine officers and two NCOs were pulled from the 1st MarDiv's own three-quarters completed scout course being conducted in Australia and assigned to the Amphibious Scout School along with three Seventh Amphibious Force officers and six enlisted (all with landing craft training), three Australian Army officers and six enlisted (all veterans of North Africa), three Australian New Guinea Police Force patrol officers, three officers of the 32d InfDiv, and 20 New Guinea and New Britain natives attached from the Australian New Guinea Administrative Unit (ANGAU) as guides. The officers were lieutenants and ensigns. They were to develop the envisioned Amphibious Scout School's program of instruction.

In charge of the school and ultimately the unit was LCdr William F. Coultas, a Naval Intelligence officer and scientist who had traveled through the southern Solomons between 1928 and 1934 undertaking research for the American Museum of Natural History's Whitney South Seas Expeditions. The concept of the Amphibious Scouts was different than other scout units. It

Amphibious Scouts of Special Service Unit No. 1 made extensive use of the LCP(R). Four were carried aboard many destroyer transports, although they were often replaced by the LCVP with a full bow ramp. Besides the narrow bow ramp, the machine-gun manholes were in the LCP(R)'s bow rather than in the stern as on the LCVP. SSU #1 recon boat crews consisted of 5–7 men. Note also the stacked LCR(S) rubber boats.

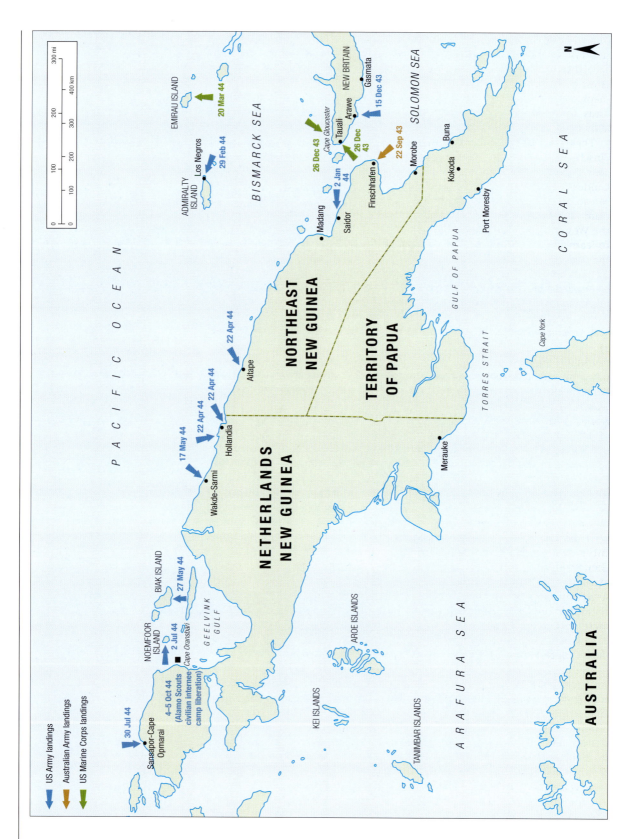

Special Service Unit No.1's pre-landing reconnaissance missions on New Guinea. Landings prior to September 1943 are not shown.

relied on natives intimately familiar with the area of operations, but without military experience, to guide and provide their bush skills for military specialists trained in technical reconnaissance. The teams would study the latest aerial photos of the target areas and then go in to update charts and maps, closely examine the proposed landing beaches and adjacent inland areas for the suitability of airfields, and collect information on enemy activities, defenses, and installations.

They were initially organized into four teams and assigned objectives at Finschhafen on New Guinea and Cape Gloucester, Arawe, and Gasmata on New Britain (territorially part of Australia New Guinea). An Australian New Guinea Police Force officer led three of the patrols and a Marine was assigned to each. Navy, Army, and Australian Army personnel were assigned to each team along with four or five natives. An interesting departure was for the Westerners to learn Pidgin English rather than the natives being required to learn English. This was thought to be easier to accomplish and provided the Westerners with a valuable survival and intelligence collection tool. Initially the training covered physical conditioning, hand-to-hand combat, reconnaissance techniques, sketch maps and diagrams, carbine and pistol marksmanship, jungle survival, and three hours of Pidgin a day. The Australian Police Force officers taught the latter two subjects. They undertook 5-mile speed marches, swam, and played softball. Rubber boat landing exercises included negotiating the surf and concealing them. The Scouts were formally designated Special Service Unit No. 1 (SSU #1), Seventh Amphibious Force on July 7, meant as a cover designation. In August they occupied an abandoned PT boat base at Kalo Kalo, Fergusson Island off the southeast end of New Guinea. Here they conducted weeklong ambush and patrol exercises and worked with PT boats from a nearby base practicing the launch and recovery of rubber boats. Most of the teams' mission saw them delivered and recovered by PT boat although submarines and seacraft were used on occasion.

The shoulder insignia of the Amphibious Scouts. The Army's Engineer Amphibious Command wore an identical insignia, but of gold–yellow on blue. Both were influenced by the British Combined Operations Command insignia, which was red on black.

Combat operations

SSU #1's first mission was at Finschhafen just above Huon Gulf on New Guinea's lower southeast coast in early September. Several landings were made over a two-week period by one team. The 20th Australian Brigade landed there on September 22 based on SSU #1's successful reconnaissance. Eventually the entire 9th Australian Division landed. The next operation was at Cape Gloucester, New Britain later in the month. The 11-day mission collected extensive information and permitted I Marine Amphibious Corps (IMAC) to select Borgen Bay as the most suitable landing site. Another mission was conducted on Cape Gloucester in late November. The 1st MarDiv was landed there on December 26. SSU #1 reconnoitered Arawe on New Britian's south coast where the 112th Cavalry landed on December 15 as a diversion for the Cape Gloucester landing.

Marine Maj Melvin. G. Brown took command of SSU #1 in early November and the base was moved to Dowa Dowa at Milna Bay on New Guinea's southeast end. This collocated it with Seventh Amphibious Force, its flag aboard the USS *Blue Ridge* (AGC-2) from December 1943 to June 1945. During Brown's command there were serious disagreements with the Australian personnel on training and employment, and the Australians and natives were subsequently reassigned. On January 1, 1944 SSU #1 was redesignated the Seventh Amphibious Force Scouts. The Scouts conducted pre-landing reconnaissance for nine landings on New Guinea's north coast and the Bismarcks into July 1944.

Cape Sansapor on the Vogelkop Peninsula at the west end of Netherlands New Guinea was one of the most extensively reconnoitered landing beaches. On the other hand the September 15, 1944 Morotai Island landing by the 32d InfDiv was not reconnoitered. The beaches were mud flats and the operation could have been a disaster if it had been opposed. The Seventh Amphibious

Force Scouts' last mission as a joint organization was the October 20, 1944 Leyte landing by XXIV Corps in the Philippines (described in the 6th Ranger Battalion section). Maj C. H. Snyder, an Army amphibious engineer, replaced LtCol Brown.

1945 changes
In late January 1945 the nature of the unit changed. There were numerous administrative and operational problems associated with the joint unit, and so all non-Navy personnel were returned to their parent service and the unit became solely a Navy operation. LCdr J. W. Rodes, a Seventh Amphibious Force intelligence officer, took command. The unit still conducted pre-landing beach reconnaissance, but a team would then work with the Navy beachmaster for the first three days after the landing. Teams of one officer and two enlisted were employed. The Scouts would guide in the assault waves, take offshore soundings, blow up beach obstacles, buoy channels, and erect beach marker panels. Training was now conducted at the Beach Party Training Camp at Hollandia, Netherlands New Guinea, but operational control was still vested in the Seventh Amphibious Force's Intelligence Section.

To man the revamped unit graduates of the Navy's Amphibious Scout and Raider School were assigned from late 1944. Besides the Seventh Amphibious Force Scouts, graduates of this school were assigned to UDTs and Naval Combat Demolition Units; Naval Group, China; and other organizations requiring amphibious-trained scouts and intelligence personnel.

The Amphibious Scout and Raider School
The Scouts and Raiders were an outgrowth of Amphibious Corps, Atlantic Fleet joint Scout-Observer Group when the Marine Corps and Army separated their joint effort in August 1942 because of doctrinal disagreements, training methodology issues, and command personalities. The Marines preferred daylight landings with massive pre-landing naval and air bombardment. The Army insisted on night landings, which proved impractical. Selected Navy landing craft crewmen were undertaking training at Amphibious Training Base, Solomons Island in Chesapeake Bay, MD (not to be confused with the Pacific Solomon Islands) to serve as guide boats for night landings. With the departure of the Marines, it was decided that a joint Army and Navy school was needed to train men for beach reconnaissance. The Amphibious Scout and Raider School (Joint) was established at Amphibious Training Base, Little Creek, MD on August 15, 1942. Little Creek's cold waters and other conditions were unsuitable for training, but Fort Pierce, FL was ideal and the school moved south in January 1943. On January 26 Amphibious Training Base, Fort Pierce was commissioned.

Army divisional cavalry reconnaissance troops received amphibious scout training there in four-week courses. An eight-week course was begun in March for Navy personnel to become the school's core. It included a rigorous physical fitness program emphasizing teamwork, hand-to-hand combat, seamanship, navigation, small-craft engines, weapons, rubber boats, swimming, hydrographic survey, beach reconnaissance, first aid, survival, infiltration exercises ashore eluding patrols and sentries, voice and Morse Code radio operation, and signaling and beach marking with semaphore flags and lights. Much of the training was conducted at night and concentrated on operating LCP(R)s for scouting and delivering small parties ashore. In May the course was extended to 12 weeks with the addition of extensive demolition training.

In December the Army course ceased and the Army cadre and instructors were reassigned by February 1944. "(Joint)" was dropped from the school's designation. In March 1945 the name was changed to the Amphibious Scout School and it began training scouts for Naval Group, China, a clandestine organization assisting the Nationalist Chinese. It closed in September 1945.

The Seventh Amphibious Force Scouts went on to support the Seventh Fleet's over one-dozen landings in the Philippines and three Australian landings on Borneo, the last being at Balikpapan on July 1, 1945. A final mission of the Seventh Amphibious Force Scouts was to reconnoiter landing areas at Jinsen, Korea when XXIV Corps was delivered for occupation duty on September 8. In December the Seventh Amphibious Force and the Scouts were decommissioned.

5217th/1st Reconnaissance Battalion

Formation and training

On May 24, 1943, the Philippine Subsection was separated from Section C and placed directly under GHQ/SWPA chief of staff, MajGen Richard K. Sutherland, as the Philippine Regional Section (PRS). Col Courtney Whitney, Sr., long a corporate lawyer in the Philippines, became Director, PRS. The operation was classified and few GHQ staff officers knew of PRS's existence. PRS managed many of the communications and training activities formerly under the AIB. Administrative and logistical support was provided through the GHQ staff. PRS maintained radio contact with the earlier parties inserted into the Philippines by submarine and the few guerrilla groups equipped with radios. Not all guerrillas were under US affiliation. GHQ would have future parties sent into the Philippines through the PRS instead of through the AIB. Its operations were coordinated with those of the AIB. Another reason for the reorganization was that GHQ/SWPA G-2, BGen Willoughby, felt that the guerrillas were only of intelligence collection value and of little use operationally.

Rather than the earlier ad hoc parties, the PRS formed parties supplied by the 5217th Reconnaissance Battalion. AIB parties had established contact with guerrilla groups in the southern and central Philippines, but little contact had been made with those in the north, especially the large groups on Luzon. Being the largest and most populated island, the Commonwealth's capital, and economically important, Luzon became the focus of the PRS. In September it was decided that the PRS would send parties into Luzon and other areas above 12 degrees North latitude, a line passing just north of Leyte and Panay. They would make contact with the guerrillas and establish an intelligence net and a means of supplying the guerrillas. The guerrillas confirmed as being loyal to the US below 12 degrees North provided intelligence from that area. Some PRS parties did operate in the south, however.

While American personnel would accompany some PRS parties, it was preferable to employ as many Filipino personnel as possible for their language skills, familiarity with the area and people, and ability to blend into the

The unofficial shoulder patch of the 5217th (later 1st) Reconnaissance Battalion, Special. It had a dark blue felt background, an inner yellow border and carabao head, a red canton, and white stars. These were made in Australia and approved for local wear by US Army Forces Far East. Examples of this are extremely rare. (Robert Capistrano)

The 5217th/1st Reconnaissance Battalion special parties infiltrated into the Philippines played a key role in establishing contact with, requesting supplies for, and coordinating the operations of the many guerrilla groups. Here guerrillas are armed with a Japanese 7.7mm Type 92 (1932) HMG.

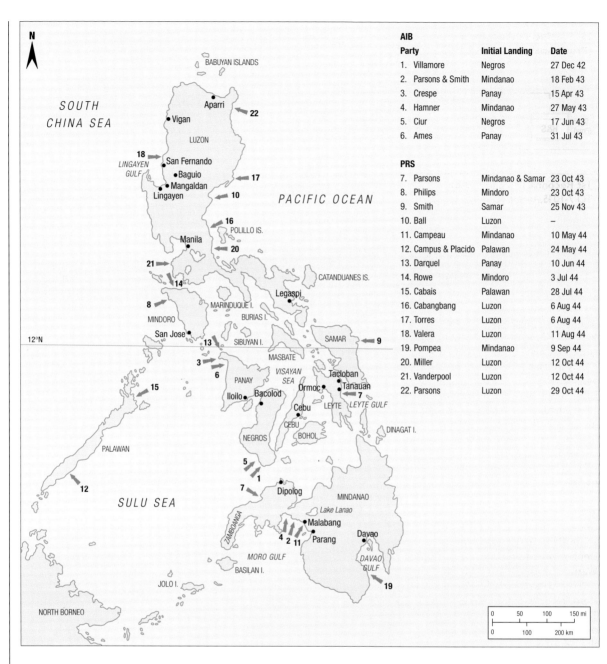

5217th/1st Reconnaissance Battalion's penetration of the Philippines, December 1942–October 1944.

population in occupied areas. (Tagalog is widely spoken on Luzon by the upper classes; 27 percent, mostly on Luzon, spoke English. Throughout the islands there were 65 related dialects, but seldom could speakers of different dialects understand each other.) The Japanese physically occupied little of the Philippines' sprawling 7,083 islands. They were found only in the cities and larger towns of economic and military importance. On many islands they seldom ventured into the countryside and the guerrillas controlled significant areas or at least moved at will.

To find qualified Filipinos LtCol Whitney visited Camps Beale and Cooke, CA where the 1st and 2d Filipino Infantry Regiments (Separate) were stationed. Both had been activated in April 1943 and were manned by Filipinos residing in the US or Hawaii and inducted into the Army. Many of the 7,000 troops were students, laborers, or field workers. The officers were both Filipino and

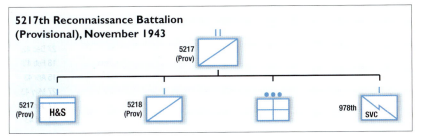

5217th Reconnaissance Battalion (Provisional), November 1943

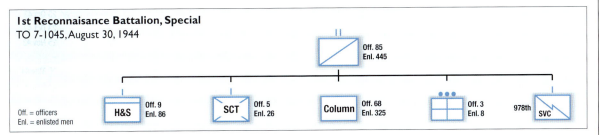

1st Reconnaisance Battalion, Special
TO 7-1045, August 30, 1944

Off. = officers
Enl. = enlisted men

American, some of whom had lived and worked in the Philippines. Whitney selected 700 men, the first group of 400 arriving in Australia in August. Prior to going overseas they first received radio operator and cryptography training at the Western Signal Corps Training Center at Camp Kholer, CA or Signal Corps Training Center at Camp Crowder, MO, plus Japanese instruction at the Army Language School at the Presidio of Monterey, CA. They were then sent to Camp Tabragalba, or Camp "X," outside of Beaudesert in southern Queensland. Here, Australia had established a training center for the various AIB organizations to include the Coastwatchers, "M" and "Z" Forces, and Dutch intelligence units.

Several hundred men for scout duty also arrived at Camp Tabragalba. They and the radio operators received three months of training typical of other special units, but with the addition of packing equipment in submarines, weather observation and reporting, identification of enemy ships and aircraft, and all had to be able to send and receive at least 10 words per minute in Morse Code. Physical conditioning took a high toll as most of the men were over 30 as immigration to the US had all but ceased 10 years earlier because of the Depression. Training was conducted at Camp Tabragalba, the Canangra Jungle Warfare School, and the Sea Warfare School on Fraser Island.

The 978th Signal Service Company was activated in Brisbane using a cadre from the 832d Signal Service Company on July 1, 1943. It soon moved to Camp Tabragalba 40 miles to the south. Radio technicians and mechanics, radio operators, and cryptographic technicians manned it and the first Filipinos from the States were temporarily assigned to the company. The unit operated a message center (Station KAZ) at Adelaide River handling all radio traffic to and from the Philippines. It also operated a signal intelligence section at Brisbane. One of its missions was to train some 110 radio operators for the PRS's Philippines-bound "advance mission," the "Mission Men." Maj Harry Croell commanded the company. Its rear echelon, those not deployed on missions, was about 200 men.

The 5217th Reconnaissance Battalion (Prov) was formed on November 6 at Camp Tabragalba. LtCol Lewis Brown, III, a cavalry officer who had been XO of the PRS, took command. The battalion consisted of the HQ and HQ Company, Medical Detachment, and 5218th Reconnaissance Company (Prov). The 5218th served as a training and home unit for PRS personnel sent to the Philippines—the "forward area." The battalion was authorized 520 men, but was habitually 80–100 understrength. The last group of Filipino volunteers arrived in March 1944. The 978th Signal Company was attached and although it was proposed to merge the company into the battalion, this never occurred. The units were closely integrated though with the signal company commander serving as the battalion XO. Both used the motto, *Bahala Na*—Tagalog for "Come What May!" New personnel were assigned to the 978th and 5218th at random for specialist training. Philippines-bound parties were assembled as the mission required, consisting of 4–20 operatives. The parties were named after their commander, usually a captain or major, who could be Filipino or American.

Combat operations: the Philippines 1943–45

Between October 1943 and October 1944, 16 PRS parties were infiltrated into the Philippines. The Philips Party, the first to be landed on Mindoro in October 1943, was virtually wiped out in February 1944. The 17-man Kopp Party was lost aboard the USS *Seawolf* (SS-197) during infiltration when it was mistakenly attacked by the USS *Richard M. Rowell* (DD-403) and aircraft and sunk on October 3, 1944 off Morotai Island. A Parachute Section was established in May 1944 at Camp Tabragalba with the aid of three 503d Parachute Infantry paratroopers under 1stLt Earl Walter. This would give the unit the capability to airdrop parties into the Philippines. However, while 66 men were jump-qualified, no parties were delivered by this means. In May 1945, 11 men, now based at Hollandia, parachuted into Netherlands New Guinea to recover three survivors of a crashed transport in which 21 died. After 42 days in the jungle the survivors had recovered sufficiently to walk to a valley and were airlifted out by gliders picked up by tow aircraft.

On 21 November 1944, the 5217th Reconnaissance Battalion and 978th Signal Company relocated to Hollandia, Netherlands New Guinea. This placed the unit and Station KAZ closer to the area of operations, although the southern Philippines was over 1,200 miles to the northwest. On November 20, 1944 the 5217th was disbanded and its assets organized as the 1st Reconnaissance Battalion, Special. The 978th Signal Service Company remained attached. Station KAZ was moved to Leyte after the October US landing.

The 1st Battalion's Table of Distribution (TD) 7-1045, dated August 30, 1944, called for a nine-officer and 86-enlisted HQ, HQ and Service Company; a three-officer and eight-enlisted Medical Detachment; a five-officer and 26-enlisted cadre Scout Company, and a grouping of 68 officers and 325 NCOs designated simply as the "Column." The Column was an organization to which the special parties in the Philippines, those undergoing training for future deployment, and casuals (personnel returned from missions) were assigned. The Scout Company was a training unit; radio operators accompanying the parties were trained by the 978th Signal Company. Total battalion strength was 85 officers and 445 enlisted, but it was about 100 troops understrength.

As the US advanced through the Philippines the PRS was disestablished and its functions split between GHQ G-3 (operations) and G-4 (logistics), both of which received a Philippines Regional Section on June 2, 1944. Both sections were still supervised by Col Whitney. This in effect placed all 83 intelligence stations in the Philippines directly under GHQ control and halted AIB activities in the islands.

Once infiltrated, the larger parties broke into teams and linked up with different guerrilla units. These teams would travel to different parts of the island by foot, carabao (water buffalo) cart, canoe, sailboat, etc., or to other islands. Besides reporting intelligence, the PRS operatives evaluated the guerrilla bands and reported their strength, background of their leadership, weapons, potential for intelligence collection and offensive operations, and supply needs. They would request the necessary supplies and coordinate their delivery by submarine. They would also aid the guerrillas in establishing or improving their intelligence nets. Some teams encountered problems dealing with guerrillas. MacArthur's policy was that GHQ would support only those units that were well organized, supported US policy, and would follow GHQ orders.

Only one group on a given island or in a district would be recognized. Other groups had to come under the authority of the recognized commander or be denied US support. This resulted in opposing groups vying for US recognition through the PRS party and even led to armed conflicts between groups. This sometimes forced PRS party commanders to take sides. Their primary mission was to set up and operate radio stations to report intelligence, weather, and operational and logistical information. Most "Mission Men" were armed with an M1 carbine or Thompson SMG, a .45-cal. pistol, and a trench knife or bolo machete.

The guerrillas proved to be extremely valuable in the reconquest of the Philippines. Filipino and US servicemen who had refused to surrender provided the guerrilla leadership. The size and capabilities of guerrilla units differed widely. Besides fighters, a great many Filipinos served as underground auxiliaries. In October 1943 the Japanese released most Filipino prisoners of war and many joined the guerrillas. For the most part the guerrillas avoided large-scale operations and direct confrontations until after the US October 1944 invasion. They mainly collected intelligence, aided escaped prisoners and downed airmen, harassed the enemy, and spread propaganda. After US forces landed on an island the guerrillas would secure landing sites, roads and towns ahead of advancing US troops, conduct more aggressive operations in the enemy's rear, perform reconnaissance, act as guides, and provide rear area security. Some of the better-organized and trained units fought alongside US units. Some 260,000 Filipinos served in guerrilla organizations and killed an estimated 8–10,000 Japanese.

By April 1945 message traffic from the few remaining teams had decreased to a trickle. As US forces liberated the islands, PRS teams reported in and assembled at Camp San Miguel, Luzon as did the 978th Signal Company. Many of the men were detached to the Philippine Civil Affairs Unit (military government) and Counter-Intelligence Corps units, and others served as guides. On July 19 the battalion moved to Manila and on August 15 it was inactivated. The Filipino enlisted men were reassigned to the 1st Filipino Infantry now at Tacloban, Leyte. Station KAZ closed in September. The 978th Signal Company was reorganized, re-staffed, and deployed to Tokyo to support GHQ until inactivated on March 5, 1946. Many discharged battalion members remained in the Philippines and others returned to the States, often with war brides.

The battalion did not receive campaign credit for the Philippines as only elements were infiltrated and not the headquarters. The 978th Signal Company received the Meritorious Unit Citation. It and the battalion received the Philippine Presidential Unit Citation. Twenty-nine men were lost in combat, in addition to the 17 aboard the *Seawolf*, plus two missing who are believed captured and murdered.

Alamo Scouts

In November 1943 LtGen Walter Krueger, commanding Sixth Army in the SWPA, directed that a special reconnaissance unit be formed to support ALAMO Force operations. ALAMO Force was Sixth Army's operational forces. Krueger was from San Antonio, TX, home of the Alamo. Influenced by the Navy's SSU #1, Krueger desired a dedicated reconnaissance unit that could penetrate inland and provide more than just coastal intelligence. Krueger was disappointed too in the poor cooperation received from the Navy in passing intelligence gleaned by its scouts prior to the New Britain landings.

The Alamo Scouts' Nellist Team after the Cabanatuan raid, January 1945. They are armed with M1 rifles, M1A1 carbines, pistols, and an M1928A1 SMG.

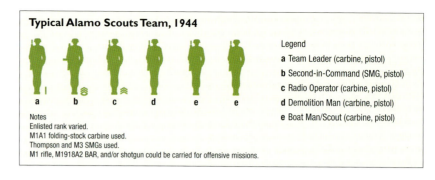

Formation and training

On November 21 LtCol Fredrick W. Bradshaw, an infantry officer with exceptional organizational skills in the Sixth Army G-2 Section, was directed to establish the Alamo Scouts Training Center (ASTC). Maj Homer A. "Red" Williams was XO. It was opened at Kalo Kalo on Fergusson Island 40 miles off the southeast end of New Guinea on December 3. The Center borrowed training concepts from SSU #1, the Rangers, Scout and Raider School, and Australian Commandos. The six-week course included physical conditioning, hand-to-hand combat, jungle survival, basic native languages and customs, intelligence collection, scouting and patrolling, navigation, communications, Allied and enemy weapons, infiltration and exfiltration techniques, and rubber boats. Candidates were selected from Sixth Army combat units through a series of interviews and were required to have combat experience, the ability to swim, be in excellent physical condition, and have 20/20 vision. There were only about a half-dozen instructors; other specialists were borrowed from the Sixth Army staff and later, team members would instruct. Class size was about 35 with an attrition rate of up to 40 percent.

The first class began December 27 and graduated on February 5, 1944. A unique aspect of the course was peer evaluation. Enlisted graduates wrote the names of three enlisted men and three officers they would prefer to serve with on a team. Officers listed the three enlisted they would prefer on their team. Instructors also made evaluations. Most graduates were returned to their units to serve as scouts and impart their skills. Fewer than half of the 250 enlisted graduates and a third of the 75 officers were retained to serve in the Alamo

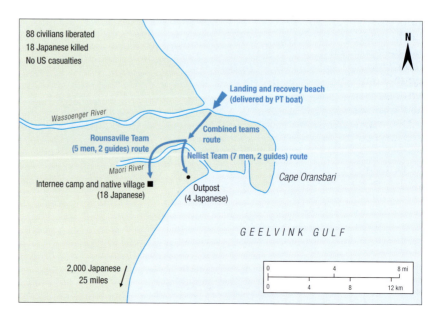

The Alamo Scouts' liberation of the civilian internee camp at Cape Oransbari, Netherlands New Guinea, October 4–5, 1944.

Scouts, formerly designated the Sixth Army Special Reconnaissance Unit. By June 1944 there were five operational teams. Twenty teams were raised plus five scratch teams for rush missions in which 21 officers and 117 enlisted served. Typically there were 10 teams and about 70 men assigned at any one time. The ASTC possessed a very small staff, a few support personnel, and men to operate and maintain its training landing craft (two LCMs, LCVP, picket boat). Convalescent personnel from other units would be detailed for support.

After conducting Classes 1 and 2 on Fergusson Island, the ASTC moved to Mange Point, Finschhafen, New Guinea in April 1944 for Class 3. In July it relocated to Cape Kassoe, Hollandia, Netherlands New Guinea for Classes 4 and 5. In November it moved to Abuyog, Leyte for Class 6. In March 1945 the ASTC made its final move to Subic Bay, Luzon where Class 7 graduated and Class 8 was under way when Japan surrendered. The teams were training for the invasion of Japan.

Normally consisting of one lieutenant and five to seven enlisted men (six was common) the teams were identified by the leader's name. There was an NCO second-in-command, a radio operator, a demolitions man, and one or two designated boatmen; all were scouts. An SCR-300 or 511 radio was carried to coordinate the recovery craft. The SCR-694 was used for long-range Morse Code communications. Standard armament was an M1A1 carbine and a .45cal. pistol. One man often carried a Thompson or M3 SMG. If the mission was offensive some might carry M1 rifles, a BAR, or a shotgun.

Sixth Army G-2 Section tasked the ASTC with a mission, a team was designated, the mission was coordinated by the G-2, and Army service units provided any necessary support. Rubber boat insertion from PT boats was the most common means of delivery and recovery, but landing craft, flying boats, submarines, and even L-5 liaison aircraft were used. The teams conducted mostly reconnaissance missions in which great effort was made to avoid enemy contact. Beaches, bays, rivers, small islands, and specific inland areas of interest were their objectives. They conducted some offensive missions including prison camp raids and prisoner snatches.

Combat operations 1944–45

In the course of the teams' 106 missions conducted between February 27, 1944 and September 25, 1945 they killed 84 Japanese and captured 24. Nellist and Rounsaville Teams participated in two prison camp raids, the best known being the Cabanatuan raid with the 6th Rangers (see the chapter starting on p.80 entitled *6th Ranger Battalion*). Prior to this the same two teams liberated 88 Dutch, Javanese, and French civilian internees on October 4–5, 1944 at Cape Oransbari, Netherlands New Guinea. Thirty-seven missions were conducted on New Guinea and the Bismarcks, 13 on Leyte, 54 on Luzon (11 conducted for Eighth Army), and two on Kyushu, Japan. While a very small number of personnel were wounded, the Alamo Scouts did not lose a single man during their 1,482 man-days behind enemy lines.

The Alamo Scouts escorted LtGen Krueger to Wakayama, Japan on September 14–25, and Sixth Army HQ was established in Kyoto. The Alamo Scouts were disbanded there in late November 1945. There was no official date, the unit simply dwindled away as men were reassigned. In 1988 the Alamo Scouts were honorably awarded the Special Forces Qualification Tab.

The shoulder sleeve insignia of the Alamo Scouts.

Alamo Scout teams and missions

Team	Missions
McGowen Team	5
Reynolds Team	2
Rounsaville Team	7
Barnes Team	1
Sumner Team†	11
Ileto Team	2
Thompson Team	9
Farkas Team	1
Ouzts Team	2
Sombar Team	4
Littlefield Team	13
Derr Team	4
Dove Team	8
Lutz Team	3
Shirkey Team	7
Hobbs Team	9
Nellist Team	8
Adkins Team	1
Chenley Team	9
Moon Team	2
Farrow Team*	2
Chalko Team*	1
Evans Team*	1
Fisher Team*	1
Roberts Team*	1

* Scratch teams.
† Sumner Team became Vicky Team to perform the final two missions.

Raider units

USMC Raiders

The Marine Corps had begun experimenting with rubber boats to land small raiding forces in 1938. The 1st Battalions of the 5th and 6th Marines were trained as "rubber boat battalions" for this role. In 1941 two individuals, LtCol Evens F. Carlson and Army Col William J. Donovan, who observed Commando training, separately espoused the concept of developing Marine units capable of conducting "guerrilla" operations. Carlson was considered somewhat of a renegade within the Marine Corps. He had served as an observer with the Communist Chinese in their war against Japan in 1937–38 and was impressed by their hit-and-run tactics against superior forces as well as their leadership and organizational styles. Of course, since he promoted similar concepts he was somewhat suspect and considered a bit out of step with the staunchly conservative Marine Corps. His ideals would probably have been ignored if it were not that one of his adherents, Marine Capt. James "Jimmy" Roosevelt, was the President's son. Col Donovan, who recommended a similar concept based on his experiences observing the British Commandos, further influenced the President. (Donovan, without knowing it, was considered by the Commandant of the Marine Corps as head of the Raider project, but major-generals Holland Smith and Charles Price recommended against it. He would later command the OSS.) Churchill too encouraged Roosevelt to consider such units. Both were captivated by such ideas and with the President's urging the Marines reluctantly created the Raiders.

Regardless of the oft-mentioned lofty political influence urging the creation of the Raiders, there was another, less-published source of persuasion. In 1941–42 several Marine officers and NCOs observed or undertook British Commando and amphibious assault training. As with Army observers, they recommended similar units; the Army called them Rangers and the Marines named them Raiders.

The Marine Corps split into two schools of thought. Many, led by MajGen Holland Smith, opposed the organization of specialized amphibious Raider units, maintaining all Marine units were capable of such operations by virtue of their training. The Commandant of the Marine Corps, MajGen Thomas

The Marine Raiders were conceived as a unit for conducting lightning-fast raids. Here Raiders undergoing training at Camp Lejeune, NC rush ashore from LRC(R)s. The man in the foreground is carrying a folding-stocked M55 Reising SMG.

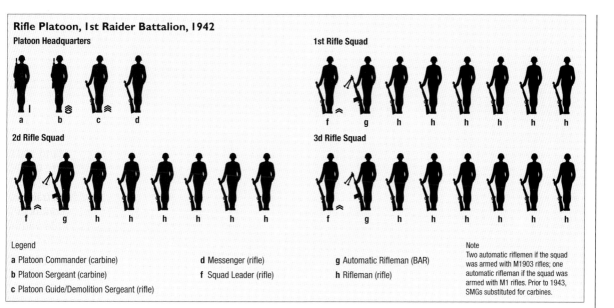

Holcomb felt the same, but bowed to pressure. The Marines still maintain this view and continue to resist the formation of "an elite within an elite" (although a small experimental Special Operations Command Detachment was raised in 2002). The other school, encouraged by President Roosevelt, felt there was a need for such units.

Holland Smith though did endorse the concept of a light strike force landing via rubber boats. This concept underwent further testing during FLEX 7 in February 1941 when Companies A, E, and I, 7th Marines (one company per battalion) were reorganized as "provisional rubber boat companies" and collectively called the Mobile Landing Group. The regiment was part of the just activated 1st MarDiv located at Guantánamo Bay, Cuba. The companies were landed by rubber boat from three destroyer-transports and executed diversionary operations and seized inland objectives to block enemy reinforcements approaching the main landing's beachhead. Parachute and glider units, also under development by the Marines, were to be used in conjunction with such economy-of-force operations. During 1941 maneuvers in North Carolina, Smith employed 1/5 Marines in a similar manner. Embarked aboard six APDs, the "light battalion" or "APD battalion," landed in the "enemy's" rear along with attached

The destroyer-transport was ideal for transporting Raiders. The transport shown here is the USS *Lloyd* (APD-63), a converted destroyer escort (formerly DE-209). The converted DEs each carried four LCVPs. They were camouflage painted for hiding along shores and blending into shorelines of nearby islands they were passing, thus making it difficult for submarines to detect them.

The battle blaze of the Marine Raiders.

The Solomon Islands, 1942–43.

parachute and tank companies to attack the reserves and block a line of communications. It was proposed that the battalion be reorganized into four small rifle companies with headquarters (including a demolition platoon) and weapons companies and armed with light weapons. A division of six APDs could carry the six companies, their size restricted by the 140 troops an APD could carry. However, the Marines could not afford to make 1/5 Marines separate as additional troops to raise a new battalion for the regiment were unavailable. Pearl Harbor changed this.

These concepts envisioned light forces directly supporting the main amphibious assault, and in early 1942 the need for Raider units seemed viable. The British formed the Commandos to give them the ability to strike back at the victorious enemy and keep him off balance with pinpricks. America too was suffering defeat and needed a means of fighting back for morale purposes and to allow time to rebuild. A unit capable of executing economy-of-force raids seemed to meet the requirement, "expeditions of raid character for demolition and other destruction of shore installations." Like the Commandos and Army Rangers, the Raiders would be light amphibious strike units well suited for operations in the Pacific.

The 1st Separate Battalion was organized from 1/5 Marines, 1st MarDiv at Quantico, VA on January 6, 1942 with LtCol Merritt A. "Red Mike" Edson commanding and Maj Samuel B. Griffith, II as XO (who had observed Commando training in 1941). Edson had served on the Mexican border and in China, fought guerrillas in Nicaragua, had been an aviator, taught tactics, and was a national champion marksman. Because of the President's suggestion for

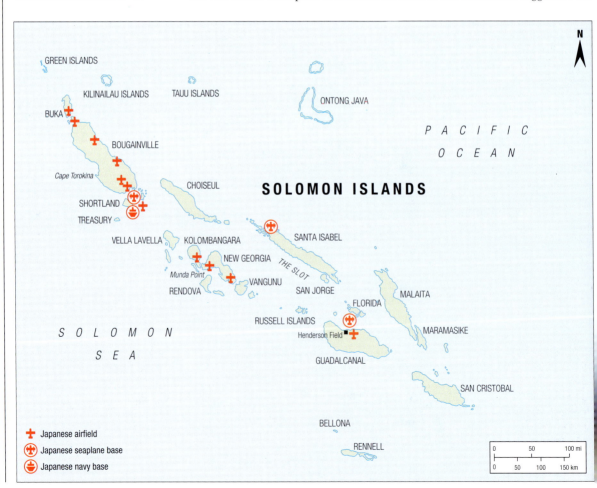

such units, the Navy approved the formation of a second commando-type unit on January 23. On February 4 the 2d MarDiv at San Diego activated the 2d Separate Battalion (following the British lead as Commando units had initially been designated "independent companies"). One-third of 1st Battalion was sent as cadre for the 2d. The CO was LtCol Evans F. Carlson with Capt James Roosevelt as XO (promoted to major in May). Carlson's methodology was based on Communist Chinese precepts and included unit decisions made by collective consensus, common privileges for both officers and men (even suggesting that rank be eliminated), ethical indoctrination, limited liberty, isolation from other units at Camp Elliot, adoption of the Chinese motto, "Gung Ho!" ("Work Together"), and he expected Americans to live on a rice and bacon ration cooked individually in the field (this ill-conceived idea was soon dropped). Edson on the East Coast encouraged initiative and responsibility in decision-making by leaders. Training differed drastically. Carlson rejected many of the cadre Edson sent. The two units were as dissimilar as salt and pepper.

At the suggestion of MajGen Charles F. B. Price, commanding 2d MarDiv, the 1st and 2d Separate Battalions were redesignated "Raider" on February 16 and 19, respectively. They were soon assigned to Amphibious Corps, Atlantic and Pacific Fleets, respectively. The proposed organization for the light battalion was adopted, although there were differences between the two battalions.

Looking northwest on Edson's or Bloody Ridge, Guadalcanal after the bitter battle. The far knoll (Hill 120, aka Hill 2) is the position the Raiders and paratroopers fell back to on the night of September 13, 1942. Henderson Field lies beyond the background trees.

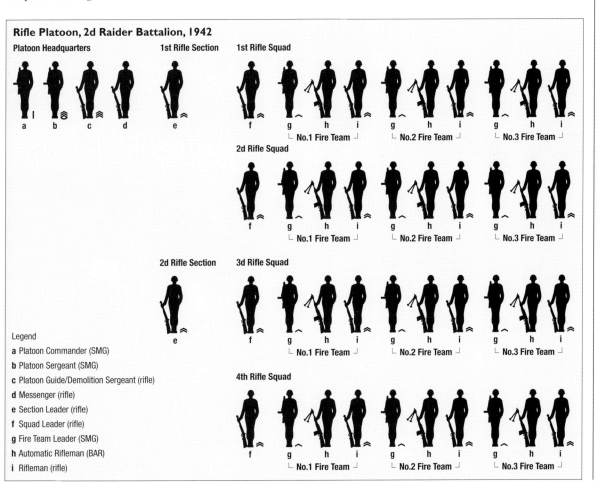

Rifle Platoon, 2d Raider Battalion, 1942

Legend
a Platoon Commander (SMG)
b Platoon Sergeant (SMG)
c Platoon Guide/Demolition Sergeant (rifle)
d Messenger (rifle)
e Section Leader (rifle)
f Squad Leader (rifle)
g Fire Team Leader (SMG)
h Automatic Rifleman (BAR)
i Rifleman (rifle)

The parent divisions provided volunteers, of which there was no shortage because of promises of being the first to fight. The rapidly expanding divisions though only reluctantly gave up experienced troops because there simply were not enough as new regiments and other units were raised. The 1st Battalion ("Edson's Raiders") continued with the light infantry concept of swift strikes and was prepared to execute both special and conventional missions. Greater emphasis was placed on rubber boat training and achieving a march speed of 7 miles per hour (normal infantry speed is 4). The 2d Battalion ("Carlson's Raiders") strove to train as a guerrilla force, which by definition it was not, as guerrillas require support from the local population and can blend into that population. They trained in infiltration tactics with the goal of "attainment of objectives by unorthodox and unexpected methods." There was no common training program at this time, but both units emphasized runs, speed marches, swimming, hand-to-hand combat, weapons, demolitions, land navigation, and a wide range of tactical exercises, often conducted at night.

Early Raider battalion organization

The early Raider battalions went through a rather convoluted succession of organizational changes. They were somewhat differently organized and sometimes differed in the field from what T/Os specified. Edson's 1st Raiders was essentially a conventional infantry battalion tailored for embarkation aboard the six APDs of Transport Division 11 with an HQ, four rifle (A–D), and

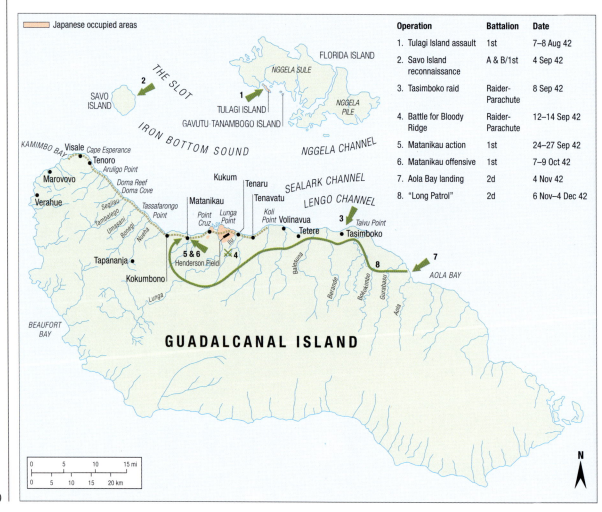

1st and 2nd Raider Battalion operations on Guadalcanal and Florida Island, August–December 1942.

weapons (E) companies—one company per APD. The battalion was initially formed under a provisional T/O developed by Edson. An official T/O, D-175, was approved on February 12, 1942 and closely followed Edson's with minor changes, the most notable being the addition of an undesired 81mm mortar platoon (no room aboard APDs). The T/O called for 36 officers and 851 Marine enlisted plus two Navy surgeons and 20 medical enlisted. Only the 1st Raiders was organized under this structure.

The rifle platoons had a five-man HQ and the three rifle squads each had eight men armed with two BARs if armed with M1903 rifles or one BAR if with M1 rifles plus an M1903 sniper rifle. Specified individual weapons were the M1 rifle and M1 carbine, but initially M1903 rifles and Reising SMGs were substituted. The weapons platoon had two M1919A4 LMGs, two 60mm M2 mortars, and two Boys AT rifles.

In the weapons company the two machine gun platoons each had four M1919A4 LMGs, the 60mm platoon had three mortars, and the 81mm platoon had four. Oddly, as it was not found in other units' mortar platoons, the mortar and ammunition squad leaders were armed with BARs for local defense. The AT section was the same as the rifle company's.

The battalion was designed to allow for a rear echelon, which remained aboard the APDs for short-duration operations. This included the battalion personnel, supply, and casual sections plus the company supply sections detailed to the Bn-4. The quartermaster and motor transport platoon remained aboard the cargo ship (AK) with the unit's heavy equipment, camp stores, additional supplies, and vehicles: two 2.5-ton cargo trucks, one 1-ton cargo trailer, one 300-gal. water trailer, four 1-ton recon trucks, and twelve 0.25-ton jeeps. The casual section maintained a pool of replacements in the form of six

The Tulagi assault, August 7–8, 1942.

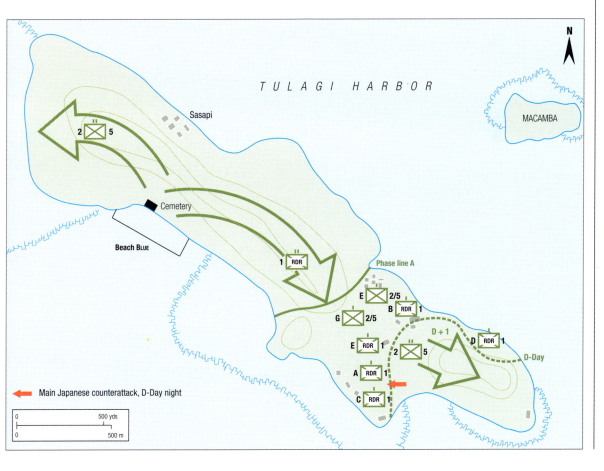

Destroyer-transports—APD

The concept of converting World War I "flush-deck," "four-stack" destroyers was suggested in 1937 to ease the shortage of amphibious transports and provide fast transports, their official classification, to move small landing parties to Caribbean trouble spots. They also had the advantage of providing fire support to the landing force. The USS *Manley* (DD-74) was the first of 26 old destroyers converted in 1938 (APD-1 to 6) (pictured). APD-7 to 25, 29, and 31 to 36 were converted after Pearl Harbor. Two boilers, two stacks, and the torpedo tubes were removed; troop compartments for 140 men installed in the empty boiler spaces and elsewhere, and four LCP(R)s were provided. Armament was three 3-in, two 40mm, and five 20mm guns. In 1943, 54 new destroyer escorts (DE) began conversion to fast transports (APD-37 to 74, 87 to 136). These could carry 162 troops and a small quantity of ammunition, vehicle fuel, and general cargo. Up to two 1-ton trucks and six jeeps could be carried as stern deck cargo. They had four LCVPs and were armed with a 5-in, three twin 40mm, and six 20mm guns. Both types retained depth charge racks. The early "flush-deckers" had a 101-man crew and the converted DEs a crew of 203. Both had a top speed of 24 knots. APDs proved to be extremely valuable in the Pacific for transporting scouts, Raiders, Rangers, and UDTs.

1st Raider Battalion, 1942	
HQ Company	9 off. 128 enl. (+ 2 off. 10 enl. USN)
Battalion HQ	7 off. 71 enl. (+ 2 off. 10 enl. USN)
HQ Section	5 off. 7 enl. (+ 2 off. 10 enl. USN)
Intelligence Section	12 enl.
Personnel Section	1 off. 6 enl.
Supply Section	15 enl.
Casual Section	1 off. 31 enl.
Communication Platoon	1 off. 22 enl.
Platoon HQ	1 off. 2 enl.
Message Ctr & Messenger Sec	4 enl.
Wire Section	7 enl.
Radio, Visual & Panel Section	9 enl.
QM & Motor Transport Platoon	1 off. 35 enl.
Quartermaster Section	1 off. 10 enl.
Motor Transport Section	25 enl.
Rifle Company (x4)	5 off. 135 enl. (+ 2 enl. USN)
Company HQ	1 off. 15 enl. (+ 2 enl. USN)
Combat Section	1 off. 7 enl. (+ 2 enl. USN)
Supply Section	10 enl.
Rifle Platoon (x3)	1 off. 28 enl.
Platoon HQ	1 off. 4 enl.
Rifle Squad (x3)	8 enl.
Weapons Platoon	1 off. 29 enl.
Platoon HQ	1 off. 4 enl.
Anti-tank Section	7 enl.
Machine Gun Section	9 enl.
Mortar Section	9 enl.
Weapons Company	7 off. 203 enl. (+ 2 enl. USN)
Company HQ	2 off. 23 enl. (+ 2 enl. USN)
Combat Section	2 off. 10 enl. (+ 2 enl. USN)
Supply Section	13 enl.
Machine Gun Platoon (x2)	1 off. 32 enl.
Platoon HQ	1 off. 6 enl.
Machine Gun Section (x2)	13 enl.
Section HQ	1 enl.
Machine Gun Squad (x2)	6 enl.
60mm Mortar Platoon	1 off. 35 enl.
Platoon HQ	1 off. 10 enl.
Ammunition Squad	10 enl.
Mortar Squad (x3)	5 enl.
81mm Mortar Platoon	2 off. 74 enl.
Platoon HQ	2 off. 8 enl.
Mortar Section (x2)	5 enl.
Section HQ	33 enl.
Ammunition Squad	16 enl.
Mortar Squad (x2)	6 enl.
Anti-tank Section	7 enl.

six-man squads (one of machine gunners, one of mortar men, and four of riflemen) but seldom were many available. It also trained replacements and administered detached, hospitalized, and on-leave personnel. The intelligence section had four M1903 sniper rifle-armed scout-snipers with one to be attached to each rifle company. The company HQs had three men to operate a TBX radio to contact battalion, other companies, or its APD. Navajo code talkers were employed at battalion and company levels.

It was with this T/O that the 1st Raiders fought on Guadalcanal. A slightly modified version was approved on September 24, 1942. The 1st and 2d Raiders did not reorganize under it and while the new 3d and 4th Raiders did, they were reorganized under the February 1943 T/O before seeing combat. Carlson's 2d Raiders was initially organized much differently to accommodate his concepts.

The 2d Raiders had six rifle companies (A–F) and no weapons company. The HQ company was similar, but slightly streamlined. The concept called for the rifle companies to be carried aboard six APDs with forward echelon elements of the HQ company split between the rifle companies and their rear echelons aboard a cargo ship. In keeping with Carlson's "infiltration tactics and unorthodox techniques," the rifle companies were compact and self-contained. For his hit-and-run "guerrilla" tactics a burdensome weapons company was unnecessary with weapons organic to the companies improving coordination. The rifle companies had two rifle platoons, subdivided into two sections, and a weapons platoon along the lines of the Army Rangers and British Commandos. Carlson though desired three rifle platoons, but was limited by the APDs' capacity. Maj Griffin, while Edson's XO, was more in favor of Carlson's organization. The T/O called for 36 officers and 768 Marine enlisted plus two Navy surgeons and 20 medical enlisted.

The internal elements of the Battalion HQ, communication and quartermaster and motor transport platoons were similar to the 1st Raiders'. There were two 2.5-ton and five 1-ton trucks. The communication platoon had a TBX radio as did each rifle company. Within the HQ company Carlson formed a provisional 14-man utility group of demolitions men and scout-snipers.

LtCol Evans F. Carlson led the 1st Raider Battalion on the controversial Makin raid and the 30-day "Long Patrol" on Guadalcanal. He commanded the unit from its formation as the 2d Separate Battalion in February 1942 until it was absorbed into the 1st Raider Regiment in March 1943.

2d Raider Battalion, 1942	
HQ Company 6 off. 119 enl. (+ 2 off. 8 enl. USN)	
Battalion HQ	4 off. 71 enl. (+ 2 off. 8 enl. USN)
Communication Platoon	1 off. 22 enl.
QM & Motor Transport Platoon	1 off. 35 enl.
Rifle Company (x6)	5 off. 104 enl. (+ 2 enl. USN)
Company HQ	1 off. 17 enl. (+ 2 enl. USN)
Combat Section	1 off. 7 enl. (+ 2 enl. USN)
Supply Section	10 enl.
Rifle Platoon (x2)	1 off. 28 enl.
Platoon HQ	1 off. 4 enl.
Rifle Section (x2)	1 enl.
Section HQ	1 enl.
Rifle Squad (x2)	10 enl.
Weapons Platoon	1 off. 29 enl.
Platoon HQ	1 off. 4 enl.
Mortar Section	8 enl.
Machine Gun Section (x2)	9 enl.

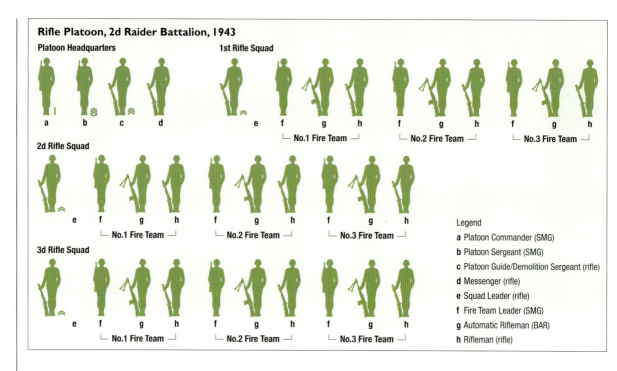

The rifle companies' two platoons had a five-man HQ. The two sections each had a sergeant section leader (rifle) and the two rifle squads each had a squad leader and three three-man fire teams. The squads were numbered 1st–4th within the platoon. The fire teams had been used earlier by the Marines in Nicaragua and China, but in this case were based on the Communist Chinese three-man cell who lived, worked, and fought together. The fire team was armed with an M1903 or M1 rifle, Thompson or Reising SMG, and BAR with the senior PFC in charge. This gave a 29-man platoon 12 BARs and 12 SMGs; considerable firepower. (Squads with three four-man fire teams were adopted Marine Corps-wide in 1944.) The weapons platoon had four M1919A4 LMGs and two 60mm M2 mortars. Fifteen Boys AT rifles were maintained in a battalion weapons pool along with four additional 60mm mortars and two LMGs. Carlson's Raiders also made limited use of Navy .30-cal. Mk 6 Mod 1 Lewis LMGs.

Combat operations: Guadalcanal 1942

The 1st Raiders (less elements) departed the States in April 1942 and arrived in American Samoa. The rear echelon remained at Quantico under Maj Griffith with Company D, elements of Company E and HQ Company. It arrived in June with the 81mm platoon converted to a demolition platoon. After additional training the battalion moved to Nouméa, New Caledonia in July. It conducted rehearsals and was attached to the 1st MarDiv en route to Guadalcanal (Bevy). While the 1st MarDiv landed unopposed on Guadalcanal on August 7 (D-Day), across "The Slot" the 1st Raiders landed on Beach Blue on the west-central shore of Tulagi Island (Ringbolt: 1,000 x 4,000 yds) at 0800 (H-Hour) unopposed. Companies B and D were in the first wave followed by A, C, and E. They were followed ashore by 2/5 Marines who cleared the island's northwest end while the Raiders pushed the enemy to the southeast end, securing the island at 1500 hours the next day. The Raiders lost 32 KIA, 7 DOW, and 55 WIA. They maintained defensive positions there until the end of the month when they were moved to Guadalcanal.

The Raider-Parachute Battalion

On September 3 the remaining 500 Raiders and 300 men of the 1st Parachute Battalion (battered in the Gavutu landing) were consolidated into the Raider-

Capt James "Jimmy" Roosevelt served as XO of the 2d Raiders under Carlson before moving to the 4th Raiders. He would be promoted to brigadier-general upon retirement from the Marine Corps.

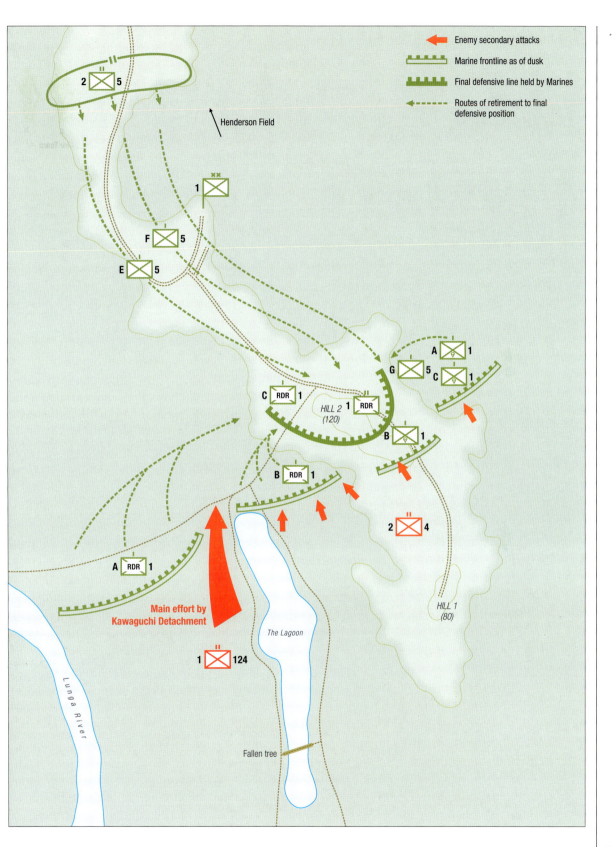

Raider-Parachute Battalion on Edson's Ridge, September 13, 1942.

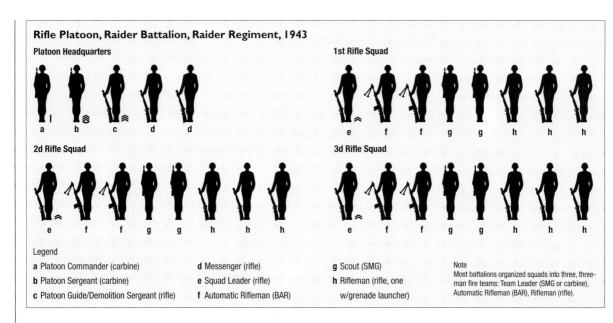

Parachute Battalion under Edson. The five Raider and three parachute companies retained their designations and rather than merging into a single unit, the parachute battalion was attached to the Raiders. On September 4 Raider Companies A and B searched Savo Island northwest of the Henderson Field perimeter finding it deserted. The next day the battalion was tasked to conduct an amphibious raid at Tasimboko 18 miles east of Henderson Field. The "Tokyo Express" was landing troops there for a major attack on the Marine perimeter. The Raider-Parachute Battalion landed east of the area at dawn on September 8. Contact was soon made and resistance stiffened. The Raiders requested an enveloping landing to the west, but 1st MarDiv could not reduce the overextended units defending Henderson Field and recommended that the force withdraw. They continued to fight on though against a rear guard, but they withdrew after the Marines gained the village and destroyed supplies and equipment. The force was extracted that afternoon after losing only two KIA and six WIA.

The raid confirmed that a large Japanese force had been landed and was moving toward the perimeter. On September 10 the Raider-Parachute Battalion dug-in on a low, grass-covered ridge on the south-central portion of the perimeter, the Raiders on the west side and the paratroopers on the east. Surrounded by dense jungle and running perpendicular to the perimeter, the ridge pointed toward Henderson Field and could have been a main Japanese attack route. Most Marine units were defending the perimeter's flanks and its beaches against counterlandings. The inland perimeter was thinly outposted.

The 2,500-man Kawaguchi Force conducted piecemeal, uncoordinated attacks on the night of the 12th after Japanese ships shelled the ridge. Smalls bands of Japanese managed to infiltrate through Marine platoon strongpoints. Efforts were made to clear the infiltrators in the morning, but resistance was stiff. The battalion pulled back further to the north on the ridge's broadest width (Hill 120) and prepared for the onslaught. It came after nightfall with the Japanese making repeated attacks. They created gaps and the understrength Marine companies were forced back into a tight perimeter. The position began to crumble and the parachute battalion CO broke down to be replaced by the XO. Attacks continued through the night and at 0400 hours Edson requested that the reserve 2/5 Marines be committed. Its companies moved up individually as artillery pounded the Japanese. Air strikes were called in at dawn and the Japanese effort was broken. The Raiders lost 135 men and the paratroopers 128, of which 59 were KIA or MIA. The Japanese lost 700 KIA and an estimated 500 WIA. Edson received the

Medal of Honor for the defense of what became known as Edson's Ridge or Bloody Ridge. On September 17 the Raider-Parachute Battalion was dissolved and the 1st Parachute Battalion departed having been reduced to 45 percent strength. The 1st Raiders was at 67 percent strength.

On September 20 Edson was placed in command of the 5th Marines and LtCol Samuel B. Griffith, II, the Raider XO, assumed command of the 1st Raiders. The battalion's next operation was to support 1/7 and 2/5 Marines in a sweep toward the Matanikau River west of the perimeter. The action lasted from September 24–27 with Edson commanding the three battalions. The two infantry battalions bore the bunt of the fighting, which thwarted Japanese efforts to concentrate forces. The Raiders lost two KIA and 11 WIA. LtCol Griffith was wounded and the battalion XO, Maj Kenneth D. Bailey, who had won the Medal of Honor on Edson's Ridge, was dead. Capt Ira J. "Jake" Irwin assumed command. The battalion's last action on Guadalcanal occurred October 7–9 during the Second Battle of the Matanikau. Five Marine battalions (3/2, 2/5, 3/5, 1/7, 2/7) again pushed west under Col Edson when they encountered a large Japanese force launching its own attack. The 1st Raiders was sent in for reinforcement. The Japanese attack was blunted and they lost 700 troops. The 1st Raiders lost 12 KIA and 22 WIA.

The 1st Raiders was no longer combat effective after battle losses, disease, and fatigue, with only 200-plus effectives. It departed Guadalcanal on October 13, and returned to New Caledonia.

In the meantime the 2d Raiders had departed the States on May 9, 1942 and arrived at Pearl Harbor. Detachment, 2d Raider Battalion departed for Midway on the 23rd with Companies C and D. The 6th Defense Battalion needed an infantry element for the expected Japanese attack. (Wake Island had not possessed an infantry force.) Capt Donald H. Hastie of Company C was the detachment CO. Company C established defenses on Sand Island and Company D, under 1stLt John Apergis, defended the smaller Eastern Island on which the airfield was located. The defenders experienced Japanese air attacks and a submarine shelling during the June 4–5 battle, but the 5,000-man 2d Combined Landing Force was unable to make its planned landing on the 7th due to the invasion fleet's defeat. The Raiders suffered no casualties. They returned to Pearl Harbor on the 22nd after performing a mission very different from that for which they were envisioned. Along with the other Midway defenders both companies received the Navy Unit Commendation.

Members of the 2d Raiders aboard the USS *Nautilus* as it enters Pearl Harbor upon return from the Makin raid, August 25, 1942. Many of the Raiders still wear the black-dyed khaki uniform they donned for the raid. Others, having lost their uniforms, wear Navy dungarees.

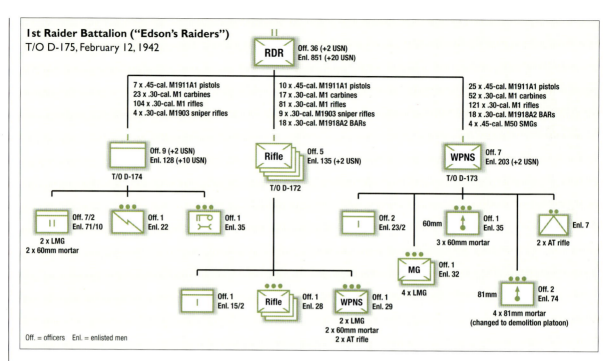

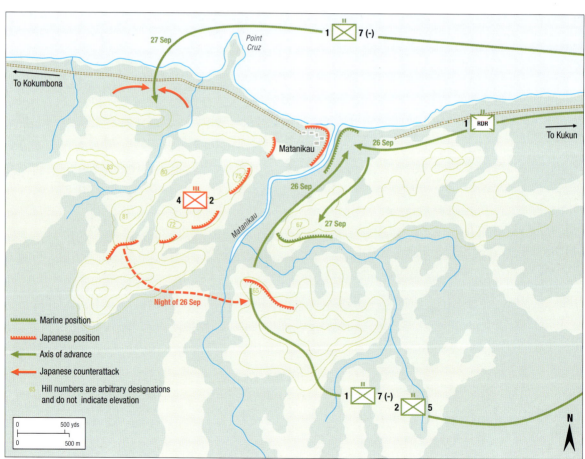

The Matanikau action, September 24–27, 1942.

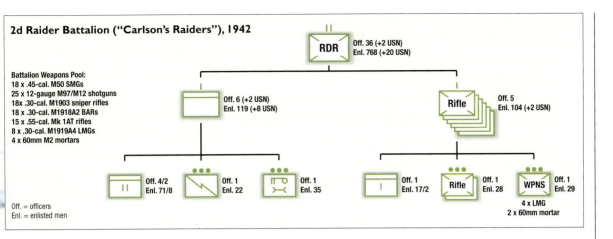

Makin Atoll, 1942

The rest of the battalion completed its training on launching rubber boats from submarines, landing over coral reefs, and demolitions. Adm Nimitz directed Carlson to study the possibility of conducting raids on Attu in the Aleutians (occupied during the Battle of Midway), Tulagi across from Guadalcanal prior to the upcoming landing, Hokkaido in the Home Islands, Tinian in the Marianas, and Wake (captured in December). However, Makin Atoll in the Gilberts was selected to create a diversion for the Guadalcanal landing occurring 10 days earlier over 1,000 miles to the southwest, destroy the seaplane base and radio station, take prisoners, collect intelligence, and divert reinforcements. After landing on the atoll's main island, Butaritari (aka Makin Island), the Raiders would land on Little Makin Atoll 4 miles to the north of Makin Atoll.

After conducting rehearsals a small battalion command group, Company A, 1stLt Merwyn C. Plumley, and 18 Company B men were embarked aboard the USS *Argonaut* (APS-1) (129 men) and Company B, Capt Ralph H. Coyt, aboard

The Matanikau offensive, October 7–9, 1942.

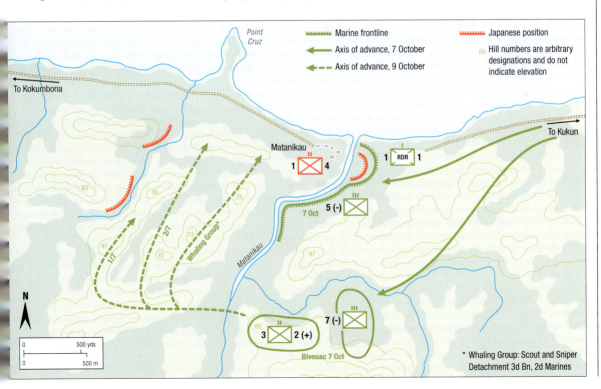

LtCol Carlson and some of his Raiders pose with trophies captured on Makin. Two 6.5mm Type 96 (1936) LMGs are displayed.

the USS *Nautilus* (102 men) on August 8 as Task Group 7.15. Because of space limitations each company left a rifle section behind.

The Raiders landed in 20 LCR(L)s at 0530, August 17 on Beach Z on the south shore and northeast of the Japanese base. In the 500yd trip boats capsized in the heavy surf, weapons were lost, and the Raiders landed widely scattered amid a great deal of confusion. Company A took the lead and headed for the Japanese base with Company B following. A firefight ensued and Sgt Clyde Thomason died directing fire and became the first enlisted Marine in World War II to win the Medal of Honor. The Japanese defenders, only 73 in number, launched two counterattacks. An air attack was delivered at 1130 hours and the Raiders downed a four-engine flying boat and floatplane that landed and attempted to take off when the Raiders fired machine guns and AT rifles. Another air attack was received that afternoon. Friendly natives provided the Raiders with information and carried ammunition. They incorrectly reported that Japanese reinforcements had landed. In the morning the *Nautilus* sank a small steamer and gunboat in the lagoon by indirect fire over the island. Maj Roosevelt recommended withdrawing as planned that night rather then attempting to advance and seize the base against a possible larger force.

Surf conditions caused major problems with outboard motors failing, boats capsizing, and weapons and paddles lost. Only 11 boats rendezvoused with the subs. Five recovered Raiders volunteered to take a boat back with weapons and paddles, but they were strafed. Carlson, with 120 troops, including the 20-man rear guard he had forgotten about and would have abandoned, remained on the island. Many were unarmed. Holding a "Gung Ho" meeting with little input from others, Carlson decided to surrender (so much for collective consensus and ethical convictions). He did allow his men the option of making another attempt to reach the subs and about 50 did, including Roosevelt. The collective consensus concept failed as NCOs and men argued about options and sides were taken, proving there is no substitute for genuine military leadership. In the pre-dawn hours Carlson sent out the Bn-3 and another Raider to contact the Japanese and surrender. They found a Japanese sailor and gave him the note to deliver. Remaining Raiders killed more Japanese, probably including the note-bearer. The surrender party returned and reported they had found no other Japanese to surrender to. Carlson now organized his 70 Raiders and they destroyed Japanese supplies and facilities while searching for food. Much of the supplies were given to natives arriving on the scene. Four more air attacks inflicted no casualties. The Marines counted 83 enemy dead and reported they may have killed up to 160. They contacted the subs and by 2300 hours the remaining Raiders in four rubber boats and a canoe were aboard having made it out on the surf-free lagoon side. Prior to departing,

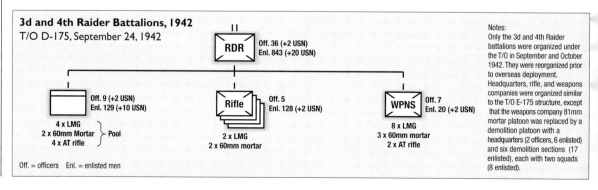

Carlson's staff plan the next steps in one of the 2d Raiders' patrol bases during the "Long Patrol." Two companies remained in the camp, which was moved every few days, for security and to allow them to rest while the other four companies conducted local patrols.

Carlson considered remaining on the island alone and organizing the natives as guerrillas. No prisoners or significant documents were captured. The Japanese implemented plans to reinforce remote bases under attack and greatly reinforced and increased the defenses of Makin and Tarawa, which had to be dealt with later at great cost.

Japanese reinforcements arrived the next day and discovered 43 KIA, 3 MIA, and 27 Japanese survivors. The Raider over-count may have included dead natives or sailors from the ships sunk in the lagoon who struggled ashore. The Raiders lost 18 KIA (seven drowned), 12 MIA, and 16 WIA. All the dead were left on the island and the Japanese reported finding "21 bodies, 5 rubber boats, 15 machine guns [BAR], 3 rifles [M1903], 24 automatic rifles [M1], and 350 grenades." After the war it was learned that nine Raiders had landed on another part of the island. Unable to link up, they hid out until surrendering on August 30 and were executed on Kwajalein on October 16. While the raid boosted morale at home as did Doolittle's Tokyo raid, the Raiders attempted no similar submarine-delivered raids. The remains of 18 Raiders buried by natives—Carlson paid them to do so—were recovered and identified in 2000. The three buried by the Japanese were not found. A search was made for the murdered Raiders on Kwajalein in 2002, but none were found.

Returned to Pearl Harbor on August 25, the battalion trained hard implementing the lessons learned and underwent a minor reorganization. The rifle section concept was dropped and the platoons reorganized into three 10-man rifle squads retaining the fire team structure. The platoons now had 36 men.

On September 6 the battalion sailed for Espíritu Santo, New Hebrides arriving on the 30th. They rehearsed for a landing on Guadalcanal with the separate 147th

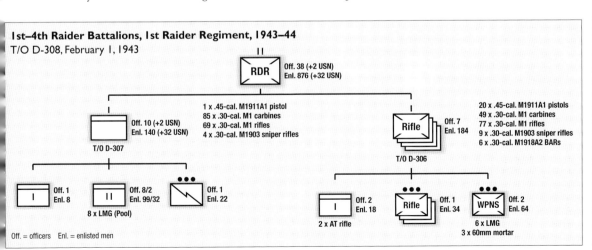

Infantry. Led by Raider Companies C and E and HQ Company, the reinforced 1/147 Infantry landed unopposed on November 4 at Aola Bay 31 miles east of Henderson Field. An airfield was to be built there, but this proved impossible owing to swamps. On the 6th the battalion began its "Long Patrol," marching toward Henderson Field accompanied by a Coastwatcher and native guides.

The unit's mission was to harass the rear of Japanese units east of Henderson. Throughout the operation the companies operated in pairs as combat teams with one team occupying a patrol base with HQ Company and the other two conducting patrols. The battalion would then move for two or more days to another patrol base. Resupply was by landing craft with native porters carrying the supplies inland to link up with the Raiders. Airdrop resupply was also conducted. Companies B, D, and F arrived on the 10th and linked up with the battalion. Company D was only of platoon-size as it had been used to fill out Companies A and B. Company A did not arrive until the 25th. By the 30th the battalion was extremely exhausted because of poor rations and the operation's duration. While half of the unit went on into the nearby Henderson Field perimeter on December 3, the rest fought a last engagement on Mount Austen and then closed on the perimeter on the 4th. The 2d Raiders killed almost 500 Japanese with the loss of 16 KIA and 18 WIA. On December 15 the 2d Raiders were shipped to Espíritu Santo for rebuilding.

In August 1942, RAdm Richmond K. Turner, Commander, Amphibious Force, South Pacific, unilaterally directed that provisional regimental raider battalions be formed from rear echelons of the 2d MarDiv's 2d, 7th, 8th, and 10th Marines on Espíritu Santo. The regiments were fighting on Guadalcanal. This order was directed without consulting the Commandant of the Marine Corps. Turner felt Marine regiments and divisions had no use in the Pacific and wanted to use them for raiding only, apparently not grasping the lessons of Makin. Adm Robert L. Ghormley, Commander, South Pacific Force, countermanded the order, but not before Provisional Raider Battalion, 2d Marines (incorrectly aka

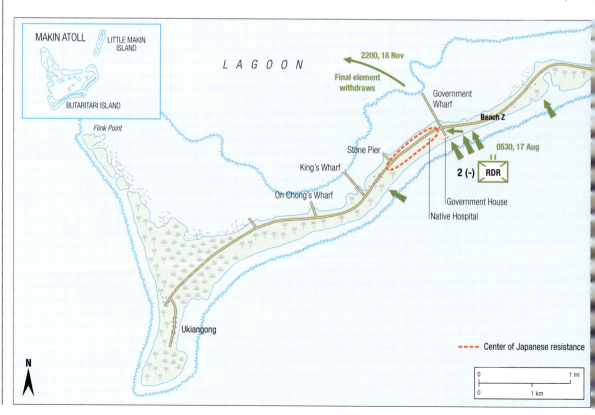

The raid on Makin Island by 2d Raider Battalion, August 17–18, 1942.

2d Provisional Raider Battalion) was raised on August 29. It was disbanded on September 28. IMAC had arrived on New Caledonia in October 1942 and the Raider battalions were placed under its control.

The 3d Raider Battalion was activated on Tutuila, American Samoa on September 20, 1942 from volunteers of the 2d MarBde, 8th and 3d Marines, and other units, plus two officers and 25 enlisted from each the 1st and 2d Raiders. LtCol Harry B. "Harry the House" Liversedge, a former Olympic athlete and conventional officer, took command. Its companies were A–E (Rifle). After four months of training it deployed to Espíritu Santo in January 1943 and then to Guadalcanal in February.

In February the 43d InfDiv was ordered to seize the Russell Islands (CLEANSLATE) 35 miles northwest of Guadalcanal to prevent the Japanese from occupying them as an outer defense for New Georgia 125 miles to the northwest. Scouts from the 3d Raiders confirmed the two small islands were unoccupied. The Division HQ and 103d Infantry landed on Banika on February 21. The 3d Raiders landed on Beach RED on north-central Pavuvu, the larger of

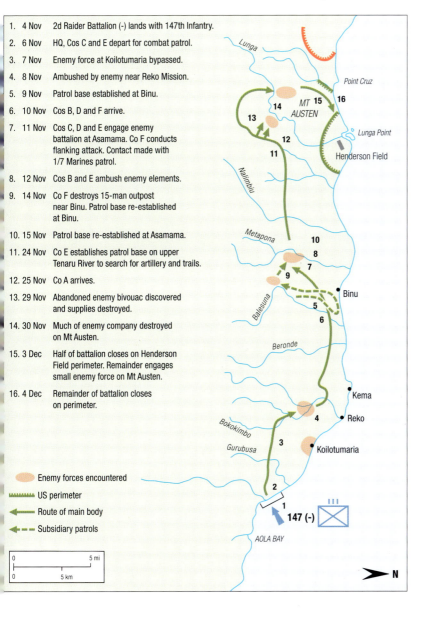

2d Raider Battalion's "Long Patrol" on Guadalcanal, November 4–December 4, 1942.

the two islands, at 0600 hours. They cleared the area and adjacent Baisen Island by noon. The next day they were reinforced by 169th Infantry elements. It was not until March 6 that the Japanese discovered the occupation. Airfields were built to support the New Georgia operation, and the battalion retuned to Espíritu Santo in late March.

The 4th Raider Battalion was organized at Camp Linda Vista, CA on October 23, 1942 with LtCol Roosevelt in command. The unit trained until departing for Espíritu Santo on February 9, 1943. It initially had only Companies A–C (Rifle) and D (Weapons). Between December 1942 and February 1943, while at Camp Pendleton, it was organized with Companies A–D (Rifle), E (Demolitions), and F (Engineer). It was then reorganized as per the other battalions and Company F provided the cadre for the Raider Replacement Training Company on February 5. On February 9 the battalion departed for Espíritu Santo. Company E was deactivated on March 22.

The 1st Marine Raider Regiment, March 1943

With all four battalions concentrated on Espíritu Santo, the 1st Marine Raider Regiment (codename BELMONT) was activated on March 15, 1943 with Col

Extremely rugged terrain was encountered during the June to August 1943 New Georgia campaign. Here coastal mangrove swamps present a formidable impediment to movement on foot.

Raider Battalion, 1943	
HQ Company	10 off. 140 enl. (+ 2 off. 32 enl. USN)
Battalion HQ	8 off. 99 enl. (+ 2 off. 32 enl. USN)
Battalion HQ Section	6 off. 8 enl. (+ 2 off. 32 enl. USN*)
Intelligence Section	11 enl.
Personnel Section	6 enl.
Supply Section	16 enl.
Casual Section	1 off. 31 enl.
Engineer Section	1 off. 13 enl.
Motor Transport Section	25 enl.
Communication Platoon	1 off. 22 enl.
Platoon HQ	1 off. 2 enl.
Message Ctr & Messenger Sec	4 enl.
Wire Section	7 enl.
Radio, Visual & Panel Section	9 enl.
Company HQ	1 off. 8 enl.

* *Five Corpsmen attached to each rifle company.*

Rifle Company (x4)	7 off. 184 enl.
Company HQ	2 off. 18 enl.
Combat Section	2 off. 9 enl.
Supply Section	9 enl.
Rifle Platoon (x3)	1 off. 34 enl.
Platoon HQ	1 off. 4 enl.
Rifle Squad (x3)	10 enl.
Weapons Platoon	2 off. 64 enl.
Platoon HQ	1 off. 4 enl.
Demolition Section	1 off. 22 enl.
Machine Gun Section	22 enl.
Mortar Section	16 enl.

The 4th Raider Battalion was delivered by APDs (in this instance the converted destroyer escort-type) and went ashore by LCR(L)s.

Liversedge commanding. A week later LtCol Allen Shapley replaced Carlson, who was in poor health, in command of the 2d Battalion. Carlson served very briefly as the regimental XO and later as the 4th MarDiv G-4. Roosevelt was replaced a month latter by LtCol Michael S. Currin. Roosevelt too was in poor health, but returned to duty on the Amphibious Force, Pacific Fleet staff.

All battalions were reorganized under T/O D-308 dated February 1, 1943 with 38 officers and 876 enlisted, and the companies were lettered in sequence through the regiment on April 1. The new battalion was based on Edson's concept, but retained Carlson's notion of no weapons company. Rifle companies had a robust weapons platoon though.

The rifle platoons retained the five-man HQ. The three rifle squads each had 10 men with no provision for fire teams, but most battalions organized their squads into fire teams with a squad leader and three teams, each with a leader (carbine or SMG), BAR-man, and rifleman. While the FMF had been equipped with M1 rifles and carbines, the M1903 rifle was still in limited use.

The weapons platoon's machine gun section had three two-squad sections, each with seven men armed with an M1941 Johnson LMG, although the M1919A4 LMG appears to have been more commonly used (eight in the battalion weapons pool). The mortar section had three five-man 60mm squads, which could be substituted by 81mm mortars from the regimental weapons pool. The demolition section had a five-man headquarters and three six-man squads. The section doubled as an engineer element and had two M1A1 flamethrowers.

The new 191-man companies exceeded the capacity of the early flush-deck APDs, but the new APDs converted from destroyer escorts could accommodate 164 troops, enough to carry a company's forward echelon. The motor transport section had two 2.5-ton cargo trucks, one 1-ton cargo trailer, one 300-gal. water trailer, one 1-ton light repair truck, four 1-ton recon trucks, and 12 0.25-ton jeeps.

Raider Regimental HQ Company	
Regimental HQ	16 off. 110 enl. (+ 5 off. 7 enl. USN)
Company HQ Section	1 off. 19 enl.
Intelligence Section	3 off. 5 enl.
Pay Section	2 off. 9 enl.
Supply Section	2 off. 37 enl.
Communication Platoon	1 off. 26 enl.

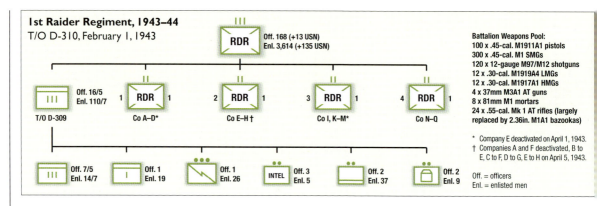

The 1st Raider Regiment was organized as a light infantry unit with its battalion capable of conducting independent amphibious raids, reconnaissance-in-force, and other economy-of-force missions as well as conventional operations if necessary. It had 168 officers, 3,614 enlisted and 13 Navy officers and 135 sailors. The regimental HQ company was leaner than its infantry counterpart. It had two 2.5-ton cargo trucks, one 1-ton recon truck, two 1-ton greasing trailers, one 1-ton cargo trailer, and two jeeps.

The HQ company's supply section held a considerable pool of weapons for issue to rifle and weapons platoons as necessary. The heavier weapons allowed the battalions to perform conventional missions.

In August 1943 the Raider Replacement Training Company was redesignated the Raider Training Battalion at Camp Pendleton with a cadre of 10 officers and 41 enlisted. Prior to the formation of the company, Raider battalions

The seizure of the Russell Islands, February 21, 1943.

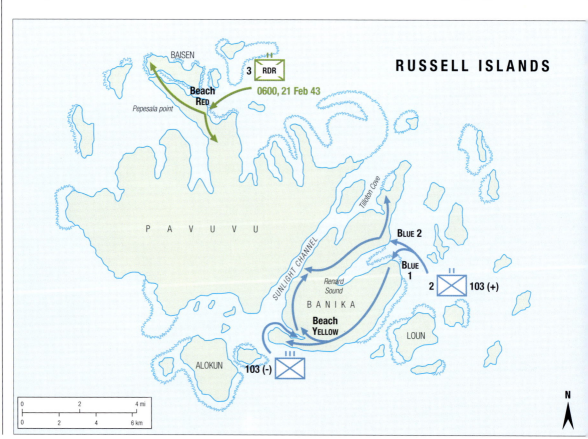

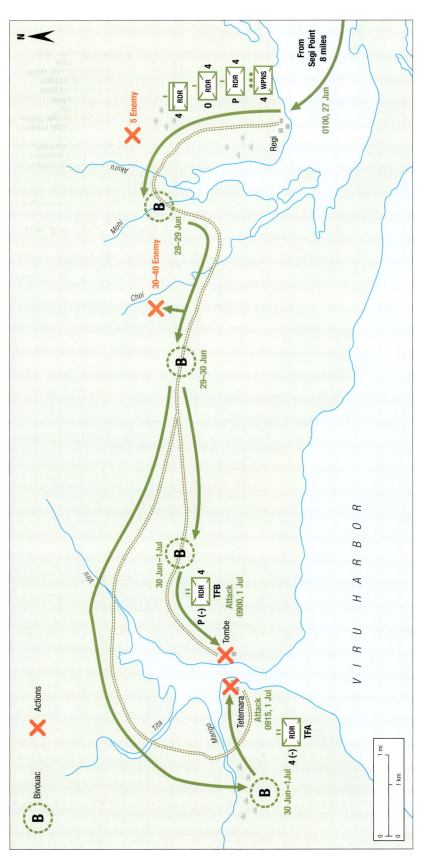

The seizure of Viru Harbor by 4th Raider Battalion (less elements), June 28–July 1, 1943.

recruited volunteers from infantry units. This led to resistance on the part of commanders having to give up their best and most experienced troops. To prevent a drain from conventional units, Raiders were recruited from recruit training centers. This also allowed combat-depleted battalions to be quickly rebuilt with trained Raiders. The eight-week training course weeded out the less fit and less motivated. Instruction included intense physical conditioning, forced marches, land navigation, weapons, hand-to-hand combat, scouting, patrolling, raid tactics, fieldcraft, and rubber boats.

New Georgia operations, 1943

The Army's XIV Corps was tasked to seize the New Georgia Group (APERIENT) 180 miles northeast of Guadalcanal. The group consists of 11 main islands and is 150 miles long and 40 miles wide. The Japanese had several small and large concentrations of troops scattered through the hilly and densely jungled islands. The operation would consist of a number of Army and Marine landings throughout the islands, but the focus was to seize the airstrip at Munda Point on New Georgia Island's southwest end. In preparation each of the Raider battalions sent a three-man patrol to reconnoiter eastern New Georgia between March 21 and April 10. Never detected by the Japanese, they collected a great deal of intelligence.

Raider operations were conducted in support of the Army's Western Landing Force operation at Munda Point, which sucked in seven infantry regiments of the 43d, 37th, and 25th InfDivs between July 2 and August 4. Prior to the June 30 (D-Day) landing on adjacent Rendova Island, the Raiders, as part of the Eastern Landing Force, first secured positions on eastern New Georgia. The 4th Battalion had moved to Guadalcanal in preparation at the beginning of June.

On June 17, information was received that a Japanese unit was moving toward Segi Point from Viru Harbor on eastern New Georgia. Fearing Segi Point would be occupied resulting in the loss of the planned airfield site, half of the 4th Battalion (HQ Company [-], Companies O and P, Weapons Platoon of Company Q; about 500 troops) was sent immediately to seize and hold Segi until Army troops arrived. The Raiders landed at 0550 hours, June 21 and were met by Coastwatchers. The Japanese were at nearby Lambeti. The Raiders paddled rubber boats to Regi Plantation on June 27 and moved overland to seize Viru Harbour on July 1. There they forced the surviving Japanese to withdraw. On June 30 the Viru Occupation Force, the reinforced 1/103 Infantry, arrived off of Viru, 12 miles west of Segi Point, to await the Raiders' capture of Viru. Because of the delay the company was landed at Segi Point and followed the Raiders overland to relieve them at Viru on July 4. The Raiders lost 14 KIA and 16 WIA and were shipped to Guadalcanal on July 8. Work on the Segi airfield began immediately and it was soon operational.

The remainder of the Eastern Landing Force departed Guadalcanal on June 29 as planned to land at Oleana Bay on the southeast side of Vangunu Island at 0630 hours on June 30. Half of the 4th Battalion (HQ Detachment and Companies N and Q [-]; 368 troops) and the reinforced 2/103 Infantry moved 2 miles east to Kaeruka and Vara villages near Wickham Anchorage. The Japanese force was virtually wiped out after four days of fighting with light US casualties. This portion of

The New Georgia campaign took a heavy toll on the 1st and 4th Raiders. By the campaign's end, the 1st Battalion had 245 men and the 4th Battalion only 154.

the battalion lost 14 KIA and 26 WIA. After searching Gatukai Island on July 8–9, it was withdrawn on the 10th and the two elements rejoined on Guadalcanal.

In the meantime the 1st Raider Regiment HQ and 1st Battalion had moved from New Caledonia to Guadalcanal in early June. As the Northern Landing Group, backed by 3/145 and 3/148 Infantry, they soon departed for New Georgia. The 1st Battalion landed unopposed at Rice Anchorage on the northwest end of New Georgia 16 miles northeast of Munda at 0200 hours, July 5. This force moved southwest 6 miles to Dragons Peninsula to secure the flanking Enogai Inlet and Bairoko Harbor on the same day. By July 11 the area was cleared. A trailblock was established on the trail to Munda on July 8 and held until the 17th to block Japanese reinforcements from the south and the enemy on Dragons Peninsula from fleeing south. The 4th Battalion departed Guadalcanal and arrived at Enogai Inlet on New Georgia on July 18 to link up with the 1st Raider Regiment and 1st Battalion. The 4th was short 200 men due to previous actions and the 1st Battalion was of such reduced strength that effective personnel from Companies A and C were given to Companies B and D to bring them up to full strength. The Japanese had withdrawn to Bairoko Harbor on Dragons Peninsula and the Raider battalions and 3/148 Infantry attacked at 0800, July 20. The exhausted troops, without artillery support, no reserves, limited supplies, and the harsh climate allowed the Japanese to repulse the attack. The force withdrew to Enogai Inlet the next morning and maintained defensive positions there into August when contact was made on the 9th with Army troops advancing from Munda Point, which had fallen five days earlier. Most of the Japanese had evacuated by barge. The Raiders were shipped to Guadalcanal on August 24 and then to New Caledonia. Casualties, fatigue, and illness had reduced the 1st Battalion to 245 men and the 4th to 154. Combat casualties were 1st Bn: 17 KIA, 63 WIA; 4th Bn: 29 KIA, 127 WIA.

While the 1st and 4th Battalions rebuilt on New Caledonia, the 2d and 3d Battalions were assigned a mission on Bougainville. Since the regimental HQ had been decimated at New Georgia, the 2d Raider Regiment (Provisional) was formed on September 12 under LtCol Shapley's command. LtCol Joseph P. McCaffery took over the 2d Battalion and doubled as the regimental XO. The 3d Battalion joined the 2d on New Caledonia from Espíritu Santo on September 3. The 2d Raider Regiment departed New Caledonia on September 30 and conducted rehearsals at Efaté on October 16–18 where it linked up with the 3d MarDiv.

Three PBY Catalina flying boats were used to deliver supplies and evacuate Raider casualties at Enogai Inlet on July 21. The exhausted Marines withdrawing from Bairoko were aided by locals, who helped carry the wounded.

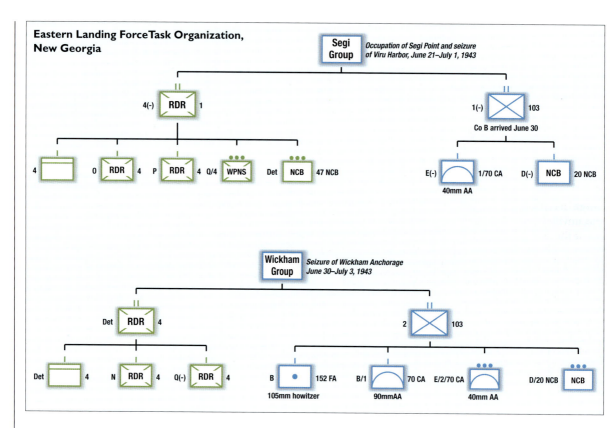

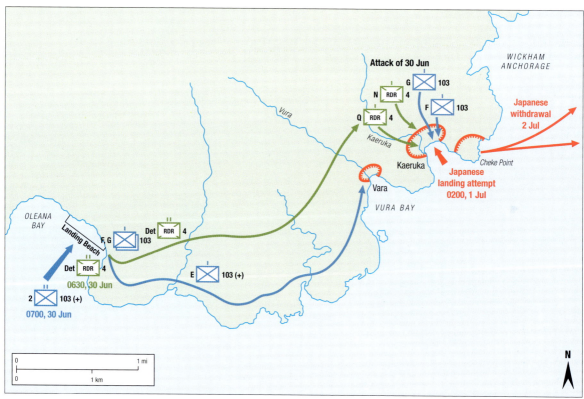

The seizure of Wickham Anchorage by 4th Raider Battalion (-), June 30–July 3, 1943.

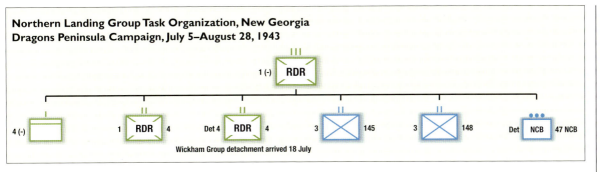

Bougainville

Bougainville (DIPPER) is 170 miles northwest of New Georgia. While geographically part of the Solomons, it was administered by the Australian Mandated Territory of New Guinea. The 38 mile-wide, 125 mile-long island is mountainous and covered by dense rainforest. The Japanese were concentrated on its ends. For this reason, the 3d MarDiv would land at a remote area on the southwest-central coast and establish airfields there. The Cape Torokina landing would take place on November 1 (D-Day). Besides the 3d MarDiv, the 37th InfDiv, arriving between November 7–19, would reinforce IMAC.

As the 9th and 3d Marines landed west of Cape Torokina at 0730 hours, 1 November with light resistance, 1/3 Marines landed on the Cape itself to rout a well dug-in Japanese company. The 2d Battalion (+ M/3) landed just to the

Northern Landing Force's campaign on Dragon's Peninsula, July 5–20, 1943.

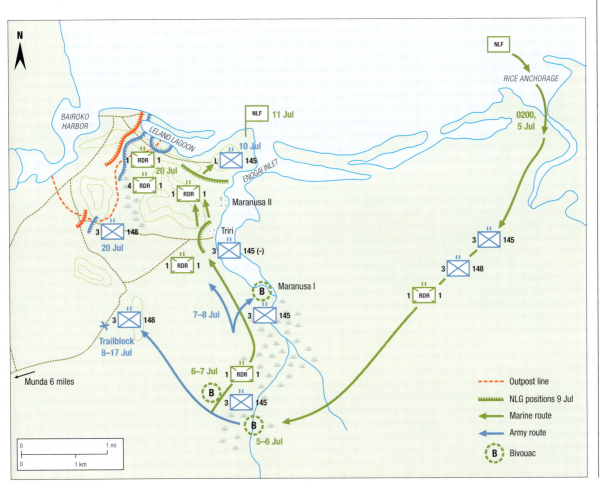

west on Beach GREEN 2. Its mission was to quickly move up the Buretoni Mission Trail and establish a trailblock on the Piva Trail to halt any Japanese reinforcements from the east. The 2d Battalion (- Company M) landed on offshore Puruata Island on GREEN 1 to wipe out a Japanese platoon. It then cleared tiny Torokina Island between Puruata and the Cape. The 2d Battalion commander/regimental XO, LtCol McCaffery, was killed on D-Day and Capt. Oscar F. Peatross, the former R-3, became the XO with the Bn-3, Maj Richard T. Washburn, taking over 2d Battalion.

The Raiders maintained the trailblock 1,500yds from the beach and 300yds outside the main perimeter by rotating companies. From November 5–10 the Raiders beat off several attacks and conducted local counterattacks. The Regiment was then placed in division reserve. For the rest of November the Raiders conducted patrols, helped expand the perimeter, and served on the line and in reserve.

M/3 was attached to the Marine 1st Parachute Battalion for the November 29 Koiari Beach raid. The force landed at 0400 hours in Empress Augusta Bay 10 miles east of the Cape. Tasked to harass reinforcements approaching the perimeter, the 600-man force encountered over 1,000 Japanese and withdrew after dark. This was the last combat action in which the Raiders fought as Raiders. With the arrival of the Americal Division, the 2d Raider Regiment was relieved by the 132d Infantry and sailed to Guadalcanal to assemble with the remainder of the 1st Raider Regiment. The 2d Raider Regiment lost 64 KIA and 204 WIA on Bougainville. It was disbanded on Guadalcanal on January 26, 1944 and the 2d and 3d Battalions reverted to the 1st Raider Regiment.

In December 1943 Headquarters, Marine Corps announced its desire to reorganize the Raiders as infantry. The "elite within an elite" was never fully accepted and the drain of high-quality troops to the Raiders hampered the effectiveness of other units. It was also felt that conventional infantry units, rehearsed and tailored, could have executed most of the operations conducted by the Raiders. The nature of the war in the Central Pacific was also changing. Heavily armed assault troops landed by amphibian tractors and supported by massive naval gunfire and air cover were needed to attack the widely separated islands on which operations now focused. There would be few opportunities for small-scale raids. Two new Marine divisions were being organized and specialized units, namely Marine Raider and parachute battalions, were being deactivated to man them. The Marine Corps had planned to reactivate the 4th Marines, lost on Corregidor in 1942, from especially distinguished units. The 1st Raider Regiment would provide the assets for the new 4th Marines. (The new 4th Marines did not pick up the Raider lineage, but that of the old 4th Marines.)

At Tassafarougu, Guadalcanal Col Liversedge turned the Regiment over to LtCol Samuel D. Puller (brother of Lewis B. "Chesty" Puller) and LtCol Shapley became the XO on December 27. On January 26, 1944 Shapley assumed command. The understrength 2d Battalion was deactivated on January 31. The rest of the Regiment was deactivated on February 1; the same day the 4th Marines (Separate) was reactivated with Shapley commanding. Most of the 700 cadre and replacements of the Raider Training Battalion at Camp Pendleton were reassigned to the new 5th MarDiv. The planned 6th and 7th Raider Battalions were canceled.

Amidst discarded Japanese ammunition boxes, men of Company M, 3d Raiders return fire on the larger-than-expected Japanese force encountered during the November 29 Koiari Beach raid. The company was attached to the 1st Parachute Battalion for the planned four-day operation, but was withdrawn the day it was landed.

1st Raider Regiment	4th Marines
HQ Company	HQ & Service Company
1st Battalion	1st Battalion
2d Battalion	Weapons Company
3d Battalion	3d Battalion
4th Battalion	2d Battalion

Almost 6,000 Marines and sailors had served in the Raiders. They had suffered 288 KIA, 20 DOW, 19 MIA, and 732 WIA.

The 4th Marines, with large numbers of former Raiders, secured unoccupied Emirau Island in March. As part of the 1st MarBde (Prov) it fought on Guam, and was later assigned to the 6th MarDiv with which it fought on Okinawa. It was the first unit to land in Japan prior to V-J Day.

Marine Raider unit commanders		
1st Marine Raider Regiment	Col Harry B. Liversedge	15 Mar 43
	LtCol Samuel D. Puller	27 Dec 43
	LtCol Alan Shapley	26 Jan 43–1 Feb 44
2d Marine Raider Regiment (Prov)	LtCol Alan Shapley	12 Sep 43–26 Jan 44
1st Raider Battalion	LtCol Merritt A. Edson	16 Feb 42
	Maj Samuel B. Griffith, II	1 Apr 42 (acting)
	LtCol Merritt A. Edson	14 Apr 42
	Maj Samuel B. Griffith, II	5 May 42 (acting)
	LtCol Merritt A. Edson	10 May 42
	Maj Samuel B. Griffith, II	14 May 42 (acting)
	LtCol Merritt A. Edson	4 Jul 42
	LtCol Samuel B. Griffith, II	20 Sep 42 (WIA 26 Sep)
	Capt Ira J. Irwin	27 Sep 42 (acting)
	LtCol Samuel B. Griffith, II	14 Jan 43
	Maj George W. Herring	9 Sep 43
	Maj Charles L. Banks	3 Oct 43–1 Feb 44
2d Raider Battalion	LtCol Evans F. Carlson	19 Feb 42
	LtCol Alan Shapley	22 Mar 43
	LtCol Joseph P. McCaffery	1 Sep 43 (KIA 1 Nov)
	Maj Richard T. Washburn	1 Nov 43
	Capt Bernard W. Green	26 Jan–31 Jan 44
3d Raider Battalion	LtCol Harry B. Liversedge	20 Sep 42
	LtCol Samuel S. Yeaton	15 Mar 43
	LtCol Fred D. Beans	16 Jun 43
	Maj Ira J. Irwin	15 Jan–31 Jan 44
4th Raider Battalion	Maj James Roosevelt	23 Oct 42
	Maj James R. Clark	29 Apr 43
	LtCol Michael S. Currin	4 May 43
	Maj Robert H. Thomas	15 Sep 43–1 Feb 44

The battle for Piva Trail, New Britain, November 8–9, 1943.

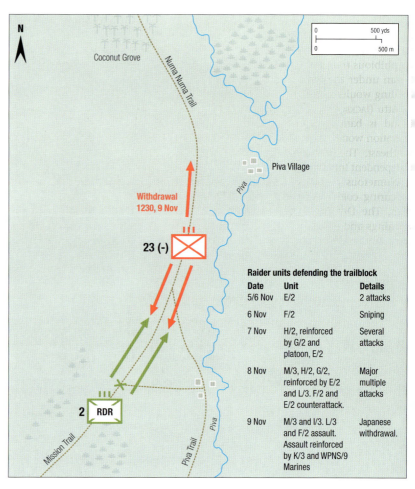

Raider units defending the trailblock		
Date	Unit	Details
5/6 Nov	E/2	2 attacks
6 Nov	F/2	Sniping
7 Nov	H/2, reinforced by G/2 and platoon, E/2	Several attacks
8 Nov	M/3, H/2, G/2, reinforced by E/2 and L/3. F/2 and E/2 counterattack.	Major multiple attacks
9 Nov	M/3 and I/3. L/3 and F/2 assault. Assault reinforced by K/3 and WPNS/9 Marines	Japanese withdrawal.

Provisional Scout Battalion, 7th InfDiv

While this unit was designated "scout" and formed from the assets of a reconnaissance unit, its one mission was an offensive operation under incredibly harsh conditions. The Prov Scout Battalion (often "Scout" was not included in its designation) was formed by the 7th InfDiv at Fort Ord, CA in January 1943. It was specifically formed for a special landing mission on Japanese-occupied Attu Island in Alaska's Aleutian Islands. The Division had been raised in 1940 and subsequently received extensive desert warfare training. Most of the troops were from the southwest US (Texas, New Mexico, Arizona) and Utah. It was planned to deploy it to North Africa as a motorized division. Not needed in North Africa, as it was apparent that Axis forces would soon be defeated there (they surrendered in May 1943), the Division was

The shoulder sleeve insignia of the Provisional Scout Battalion, 7th Infantry Division.

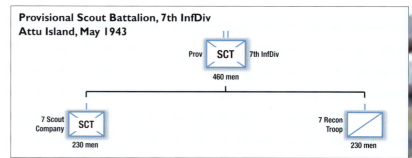

offered to the Alaska Defense Command for the Attu assault. The Command preferred the 35th InfDiv, the commander and assistant commander of which had Alaska experience, but it was scheduled for Europe. The 7th InfDiv began amphibious training with Marine assistance. Planning for Operation LANDCRAB began under the Joint Alaskan Staff at San Diego, CA in February 1943. The landing would tentatively take place on May 7.

Attu (JACKBOOT) is the westernmost of the Aleutian Islands. The 14 x 28-mile island is barren and mountainous, broken by tundra-covered valleys. This operation would by-pass the main Japanese stronghold on Kiska 165 miles to the southeast. The island was defended by 2,600 troops of the 301st and 303d Independent Infantry Battalions and North Chishima Coast Defense Infantry Unit.

Numerous problems were encountered in reorienting the unit's training, procuring cold weather equipment and supplies, and developing a realistic plan. The Division staff had some difficulty accepting the Alaskan Staff's warnings and advice on the island's brutal terrain and weather. The division commander also refused a tour of the western Aleutians to see firsthand the

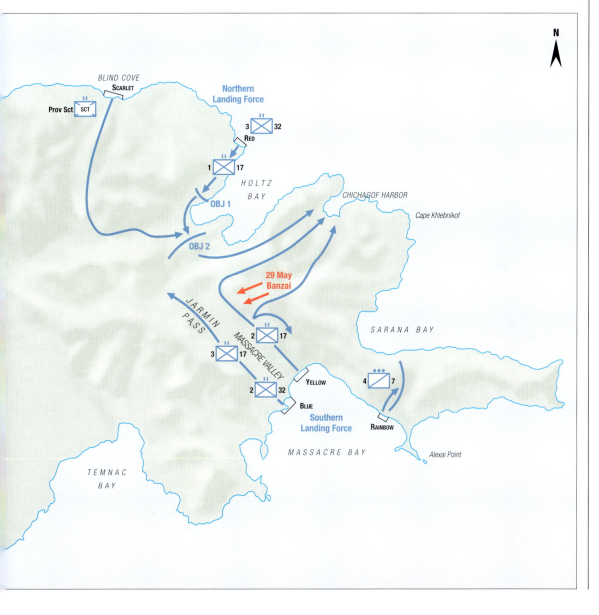

The Attu Island assault (Plan E), November 11–15, 1943.

conditions and clothing and leather boots were ordered that proved inadequate. Planning was hampered by serious personality conflicts between the different commanders and staffs, numerous misconceptions, incomplete information, and the short lead-time.

Five landing plans were developed and the final decision would be made after the latest aerial photographs were analyzed. These envisioned one or two-regimental landings on the island's bay-indented southeast end where the Japanese garrison was dug-in; and the landing of the Scout Battalion on the island's northeast end. It would move over the icebound mountains and attack from the rear, linking up with the main landing force.

The Scout Battalion was formed using the core of the 7th Reconnaissance Troop. Volunteers were accepted from 7th InfDiv infantrymen, coast artillery units, and the Fourth Army Replacement Depot with heavy emphasis on physical fitness, endurance, and experience with weapons and demolitions. The 460-man unit consisted of the 7th Scout Company and the 7th Reconnaissance Troop. Both had four rifle platoons (two two-squad sections) and an LMG platoon (three two-squad sections). Training concentrated on weapons, demolitions, rubber boats, and forced marches. Volunteers were required to maintain 4 miles per hour with full combat pack through mountains. The commander, Capt William H. Willoughby, was an athletically inclined dairy farmer with a reputation for getting things done who doubled as commander of the Scout Company. Capt Emory A. Austin commanded the Recon Troop. In many accounts the Provisional Battalion is not even mentioned, just the Scout Company and Reconnaissance Troop separately.

With limited training time and aware that they would fight a superior Japanese force, Willoughby opted for firepower. Carbines, submachine guns, and half the M1 rifles were discarded. A high density of BARs, M1919A4 LMGs, and 60mm mortars were issued and every man carried extra ammunition and grenades, to the point of sacrificing rations, which proved to be a mistake. Only armor-piercing ammunition was used for better penetration through frozen snow. A single 81mm M1 mortar was carried and used to good effect. The Recon Troop had at least two .50-cal. HB-M2 HMGs. Radios were the SCR-284, 300, and 536. The Marine Amphibious Reconnaissance Company at Camp Pendleton assisted with the unit's training.

As the 10,000-man 7th InfDiv (less elements) shipped out it was issued tropical clothing and gear. The troops thought they were bound for the Solomons where the Guadalcanal campaign was still under way. Cold weather clothing and gear was secretly loaded in San Francisco. Task Force 51 departed on April 24 for the Army's first World War II amphibious assault and the cold weather gear was duly issued. The assault force arrived at the Cold Bay staging base on the end of the Alaska Peninsula. Forced to remain embarked, they could neither acclimatize nor break-in their new boots.

The Attu Island assault, May 1943
Capt Willoughby and part of Scout Company boarded the USS *Narwhal* (SS-167) and conducted training at San Clemente Island before making for Alaska. The remainder of the Scout Battalion went to Dutch Harbor, Unalaska Island, nearer to Attu, aboard the USS *Fillmore* (APA-83). It arrived on April 26 and the *Narwhal* the next day. These men had the advantage of a week's training, acclimatization, and rehearsals. As intelligence was collected, Plan E was selected. On May 4 the task force departed for Attu even though the Japanese had been tipped off. Regimental Landing Group 17 (less Battalion Combat Team [BCT] 17-1) with BCT 32-2 attached (Southern Landing Force) was to land on May 8 (D-Day) in Massacre Bay on the south coast and attack the enemy in the Holtz Bay-Chichagof area. The Scout Battalion was to land in Blind Cove (later named Austin Cove after Capt. Austin) on the island's north side and to the northwest of the enemy positions as part of the Northern Landing Force.

The Scout Company was split between the *Narwhal* (120) and *Nautilus* (109) and departed on April 30 and May 1, respectively (Some accounts state 244 troops were landed from the subs, but they could not carry that many.) The follow-on 165-man Recon Troop (less elements) embarked aboard the USS *Kane* (APD-18). Upon arrival north of Attu on May 7 the submarines were notified the landing was delayed until the 9th because of heavy weather. The landing was delayed again until the 11th. The subs rendezvoused at 0004 hours, May 11.

The Scouts began embarking in rubber boats at 0300 hours 5,000yds off of Beach SCARLET. After difficulty locating the exact beach because of overcast and fog, a Corporal Muldanado was the first American to step ashore on Attu at 0430 hours. The rest were ashore by 0510 hours with no opposition, even though there was a small enemy outpost. The Southern Landing Force landed unopposed at 0740 hours, May 11 with BCT 17-2 and 17-3 in the first wave, followed by BCT 32-2. BCT 17-1 was the floating reserve prepared to support the Northern or Southern Landing Forces. BCT 17-1 then landed on Beach RED on the west shoulder of Holtz Bay and 5 miles to the east of Beach SCARLET in the early afternoon, having been delayed by fog. The 1,500 troops moved into the hills bordering the bay and toward the enemy rear.

The Scout Battalion began its ascent of the frozen 4,000ft mountains. They had only a day and a half of rations, having been unable to carry more through the small submarine hatches, and no sleeping bags. The temperature was 20°F. As they climbed, Navy fighters strafed their beached boats. The Recon Troop (less elements) was supposed to be landed by the *Kane* using landing craft after the beach was secured by the Scouts. Increasing fog delayed this and they were not landed until 1230 hours after being guided through the fog by the USS *Pennsylvania*'s (BB-38) radar. Most of the Troop set out after the Scout Company; some secured the beach. Rations and other supplies were dropped to the unit, but high winds blew the parachutes beyond reach. The fear of cliffs

While not confirmed, it is thought that this photo depicts troops of the Provisional Scout Battalion, 7th InfDiv struggling over the 4,000ft pass they crossed en route to attack the Japanese rear on Attu Island, May 11, 1943.

and crevasses in the pitch dark and fog forced the Scouts to halt and spend the 10°F night on the mountainside, resulting in numerous cases of frostbite. In the early evening the Recon Troop element tasked with securing Beach SCARLET surprised the four-man Japanese outpost killing two. They soon began receiving artillery fire from the southeast. The Recon Troop's 4th Platoon under Lt James Mahoney landed on Beach RAINBOW at 1555 hours on the north side of Massacre Bay to secure the east flank of the Southern Landing Force by occupying a pass leading from Sarana Bay to the north, with orders not to allow any enemy to penetrate.

At 0400 hours on May 12, the Scouts began moving and soon crossed the summit to head east toward Holtz Bay and BCT 17-1. By 0800 hours they were closing in on the enemy rear having made surprisingly good time downhill in the snow. The enemy only then discovered their presence and the Scouts began to receive light artillery fire. The Scouts attacked toward Holtz Bay while directing air strikes on nearby AA batteries. They occupied a ridge and were unable to advance further because of enemy defenses, which attempted to flank them to the west. The 4th Platoon, 7th Reconnaissance Troop, after landing in Massacre Bay, crossed the peninsula and reached Sarana Bay. It was attacked by a superior enemy force and withdrew to the ridge pass where it remained dug-in. Naval gunfire was provided and the platoon secured the pass for the remainder of the operation.

In the late afternoon on the 13th the Scouts attacked the high ground to their right front. After making considerable progress they were stalled by heavy fire from Japanese reinforcements. Casualties mounted, both to enemy fire and weather. All rations had been consumed the morning before and ammunition was low. They were still 2 miles from their link-up with the Northern Landing Force at Holtz Bay. BCT 32-3 had reinforced it that day. Col Frank L. Culin (CO 32d Infantry) came ashore and assumed command of the Northern Landing Force to include the Provisional Battalion. The Southern Landing Force was

The apparent height of these Attu ridges is misleading because of the fog shrouding their upper two-thirds. The Japanese positions were just above the fog line, which screened them but also allowed them to see into this valley leading to Holtz Bay. The Provisional Scout Battalion approached from the other side of the mountains.

having its own difficulties advancing up Massacre Valley against stiff resistance. Half of 4th Platoon, Recon Troop was moved to Temnac Bay to place it under observation and the other half remained on Sarana Bay.

By the morning of the 14th the Scouts had expended the last of their mortar rounds and were dangerously low on rifle and machine gun ammunition. Firefights were continuous and the Japanese conducted a major attack, but were repulsed. By evening half of the troops were wounded, suffering from exposure, or severely frostbit. Yet they continued to creep forward even though they had no radio contact. Withdrawal was not an option. They could not have survived the trek back over the mountains without food; nor had they the strength. They would have had to abandon their casualties. Even though the small unit was in poor condition, it fought so furiously that one Japanese officer claimed they were fighting a division. The Scouts halted their snail-paced advance at nightfall and spent their fourth below-freezing night without food or sleep. They had to keep moving about all night or they would freeze. That night the Japanese withdrew to the east for fear of being caught between the Southern Landing Force and the Scouts.

On the morning of the 15th the Scouts occupied abandoned Japanese positions with 80 men. The remaining 230 men linked up with the Northern Landing Force at 1530 hours. They had suffered light combat casualties, 20 WIA and 11 KIA, including Capt Austin. However, only 40 could walk; the others crawled. Most had frostbite and many lost toes, fingers, and feet to gangrene. Only 165 remained effective and most had bandaged feet and knees from crawling on ice. They rested, fed, and rearmed. On the 18th the Scouts were asked to patrol to the south through Jarmin Pass. Some 150 volunteered regardless of their condition. At 1430 hours they linked up with the Southern Landing Force. The Japanese were now contained on the island's northeast end.

The campaign was over for the spent Provisional Battalion, but fighting would continue until the Japanese wasted themselves in a *banzai* charge on May 29. Capt Willoughby was severely wounded in the attack and was one of the few survivors of an overrun observation post (he later retired as a colonel). Only 28 Japanese were taken prisoner on Attu. The Scout Company XO, 1stLt Clifford C. Kimsey, Jr. took command.

The Scout Company and Recon Troop were awarded Distinguished Unit Citations for their actions. The Scout Company was dissolved in June and a new 7th Cavalry Reconnaissance Troop was organized prior to the 7th InfDiv's move to Hawaii in September 1943.

The head of West Arm of Holtz Bay looking northwest. The Provisional Scout Battalion had landed on the other side of the mountains on the far side of the bay and would approach the bay from the left to meet the rest of the Northern Landing Force, which was off the photo on Beach RED to the right.

6th Ranger Battalion

With New Guinea secured, MacArthur's first thrust into the Philippines would occur in October 1944. In preparation for this, LtGen Walter Krueger commanding Sixth Army directed the formation of a Ranger battalion. The 98th Field Artillery Battalion (75mm Howitzer, Pack) was selected as cadre. (Activated as 2d Battalion, 99th Field Artillery Regiment (75mm Howitzer, Pack) at Ft Hoyle, MD on July 31, 1940. Redesignated 98th Field Artillery Battalion at Ft Lewis, WA on January 13, 1941. It trained at Camp Carson, CO and departed for Australia in December 1942.) The unit arrived at Brisbane, Australia in January 1943, but the authorities would not allow its 800 mules to land when they arrived later. The unit moved to Port Moresby, Papua, arriving on February 17 and continued training. A pack howitzer battalion on Guadalcanal had proved to be a hindrance and it was decided to disband the 98th.

Battalion organization and training

LtCol Henry A. "Hank" Mucci assumed command of the battalion on April 26, 1944, reorganized the unit under the Ranger battalion T/O&E, and began training. Mucci, a field artillery officer like William O. Darby who formed the

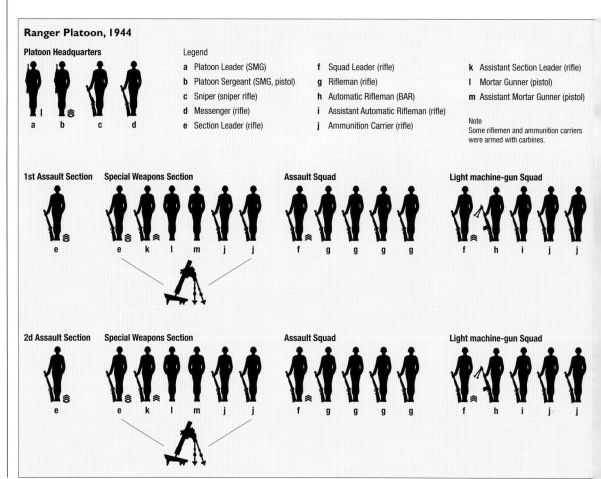

1st Ranger Battalion in Britain, had a reputation for toughness as the provost marshal of Honolulu. Maj Robert W. "Woody" Garrett was the XO. The battalion contained 900 troops and those not wishing to become Rangers or who failed the initial testing were transferred to other artillery units or the 5307th Composite Unit (Prov) ("Merrill's Marauders") and replaced by volunteers. Only 500 were needed for the Ranger battalion. Of the Ranger battalion's 31 officers, 12 were from the 98th as were about 300 enlisted. The mules were sent to Burma where "Merrill's Marauders," and later the 5332d Brigade (Prov) (MARS Task Force), was effectively using pack transport. The training program was similar to that used by the Rangers trained in Britain and the States, being based on the Commando program.

While not yet redesignated Rangers, the volunteers undertook 5-mile runs and 20-mile forced marches, and organized athletics, swimming, weapons, patrolling, and tactical training. On July 1 the battalion moved to Finschhafen, Northeast New Guinea, a staging base where it continued unit training and amphibious exercises with rubber boats. On September 24, 1944 it was officially redesignated 6th Ranger Infantry Battalion. Using T/O&E 7-86, February 29, 1944, the battalion was organized into an HQ and HQ Company and six Ranger companies (A–F). It was authorized 27 officers and 497 enlisted.

Ranger companies were commanded by a captain (SMG) assisted by a first sergeant (SMG, pistol), clerk (rifle), and messenger (rifle). The two platoons each had a four-man HQ led by a 1st lieutenant. The platoon's two assault sections were led by staff sergeants and had a five-man assault squad and a five-man LMG squad armed with a BAR. The assault sections were nothing more than 11-man squads. The company's special weapons section had a staff sergeant section leader (rifle), a sergeant assistant section leader (rifle), mortar gunner (pistol), assistant mortar gunner (pistol), and two ammunition carriers (rifle) manning a 60mm M2 mortar. The section also had a 2.36in. M9 bazooka.

The machine gun squads, according to the T/O&E, were armed with M1919A4 LMGs, but the 6th used M1918A2 BARs and rearmed the gunners and assistant gunners accordingly. Some M1919A4 LMGs were retained.

LtCol Henry A. "Hank" Mucci commanded the 6th Ranger Battalion for virtually its entire existence. He wears the sole weapon he carried in combat, an M1911A1 pistol. It was common practice in the battalion to carry pistols in shoulder holsters.

Ranger Infantry Battalion	
HQ and HQ Company	8 off. 96 enl.
Battalion HQ	7 off.
HQ Company	1 off. 88 enl.
Staff Platoon	1 off. 66 enl.
Administrative & Personnel Sec	1 off. 28 enl.
Intelligence & Operations Sec	7 enl.
Supply & Transportation Sec	31 enl.
Communication Platoon	22 enl.
Medical Detachment	1 off. 11 enl.
Ranger Company (x6)	3 off. 65 enl.
Company HQ	1 off. 3 enl.
Ranger Platoon (x2)	1 off. 31 enl.
Platoon HQ	1 off. 3 enl.
Assault Section (x2)	11 enl.
Section HQ	1 enl.
Assault Squad	5 enl.
LMG Squad	5 enl.
Special Weapons Section	6 enl.

A patrol from Company F, 6th Rangers scouts the beach at Desperation Point, Dinagat Island after securing the island and assisting SSU #1 parties install beacon lights to guide the invasion fleet into Leyte Gulf.

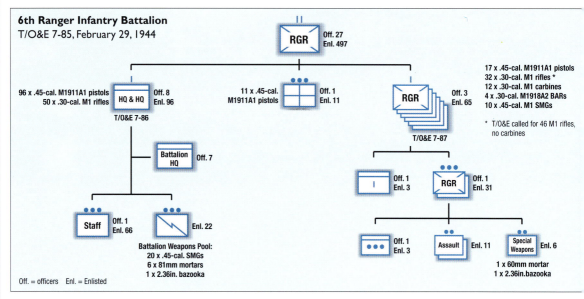

The shoulder scroll of the 6th Ranger Infantry Battalion.

As machine gunners they would have carried pistols. The ammunition carriers became riflemen. Some riflemen and ammunition carriers used M1 carbines rather than rifles, but it appears the M1 rifle was preferred. Most officers additionally carried a pistol, as did medics who also used an M1 rifle or carbine. SMGs were the Thompson M1/M1A1. Most Rangers carried M1918 Mk I or M3 trench knives. M7 grenade launchers were authorized for each of the company's M1 rifles.

The supply and transportation section maintained a pool of weapons for use by the Ranger companies if necessary (see organization chart). Although the T/O&E authorized each company two Boys AT rifles, the 6th Rangers did not use them. Each company possessed one M2-2 flamethrower. The HQ company had four 3/4-ton weapons carriers, a 3/4-ton command car, and nine jeeps.

Operations

The Leyte landings

The Rangers' first operation was to support the Leyte landing (KING II); America's return to the Philippines scheduled for October 20, 1944 (A-Day). Mountainous Leyte (CYCLONE) is the Philippines' eighth largest island and is located in the archipelago's east-central portion. To reach the island, the invasion fleet would have to pass three small islands east of Leyte to enter Leyte Gulf. There were small Japanese elements on these islands manning radar and radio stations. The

Rangers would escort two SSU #1 parties installing beacon lights on the north end of Dinagat and the south point of Homonhon between which the Central Philippines Attack Force (TF 77) would pass. Additionally, it was hoped minefield charts would be found on Suluan. Krueger preferred to employ either the separate 112th Cavalry or 158th Infantry for this mission and retain the Rangers for emerging special missions, but they were not yet available. The Dinagat Attack Group (TG 78.4) consisted of five flush-deck destroyer-transports, two destroyers, two frigates, and two light cruisers for fire support. The 6th Rangers and B/1/21 Infantry were aboard the APDs and would secure the islands. Guides from the 1st Filipino Infantry Regiment accompanied them. Rehearsals were conducted at Tanahmerah Bay, New Guinea on October 10.

A typhoon battered the approaching fleet and the weather was still extremely rough on October 17 (A–3). Regardless, the USS *Herbert* (APD-22) with Company D, 6th Rangers was sent ahead to raid Suluan Island, 60 miles east of Leyte. They would be the first Americans to return to the Philippines. Landing on Beach BLACK 3 at 0805 hours, the company moved toward the island's south end,

6th Ranger Battalion operations, Leyte Gulf, October 17–28, 1944. The objectives of each phase are numbered.

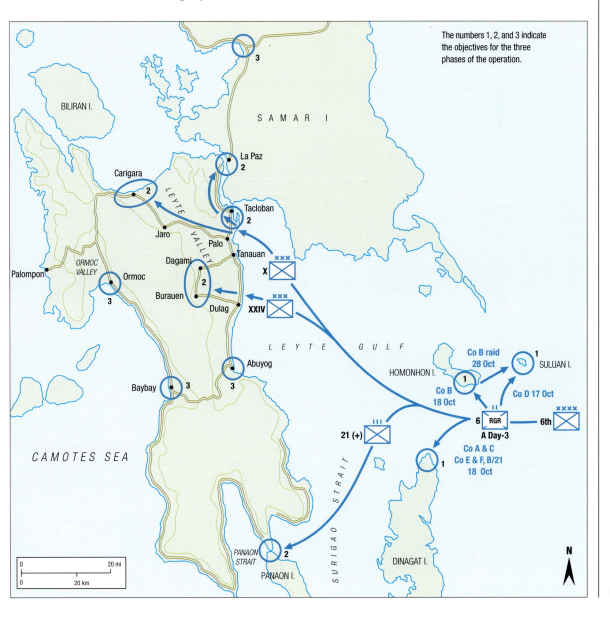

Members of Company C, 6th Rangers en route to the Cabanatuan Prison Camp on January 29, 1945. The Rangers traveled light, without packs or helmets. Each Ranger carried two bandoleers of spare ammunition, two hand or rifle grenades, 1.5 days' of D-ration bars, and one water canteen.

burned four Japanese buildings discovered en route, and engaged a small patrol, which fled. Reaching the lighthouse they found it abandoned and destroyed enemy equipment. No minefield charts were recovered. Upon withdrawal at midnight, the surf had broached the LCP(R)s and they formed a perimeter on the beach for the night. There was a brief firefight in the morning and the Japanese again withdrew. LCP(R)s from the USS *Crosby* (APD-17) soon recovered Company D, which had lost two KIA and one WIA.

On the morning of the 18th, Companies A and C under Maj Garrett landed on BLACK 1 on Dinagat Island on the south side of Leyte Gulf, the largest of the three. Guerrillas on the island had been alerted to clear civilians from the north end. Companies E and F with B/1/21 Infantry followed ashore and searched Tudlan Point on the north end (renamed Desperation Point by the Rangers). Only one Japanese was killed, and B/1/21 was returned to its ship as a floating reserve. The Rangers remained ashore.

At the same time as the landings on Dinagat, Company B landed on Homonhon Island between Suluan and Dinagat. Landing on BLACK 2, they found the island devoid of Japanese. Navigation beacons were erected on both islands as planned. The next day a Filipino reported that the Japanese on Suluan were murdering civilians and requested assistance, but the Navy had no craft available to move the Rangers. On the 20th the invasion fleet entered Leyte Gulf passing between Dinagat and Homonhon, guided by the beacon lights, and successfully landed four divisions under X and XXIV Corps.

Company B, led by Capt Arthur D. "Bull" Simons (who later led the 1970 Special Forces Son Tay Prison Camp raid in North Vietnam), was finally granted permission to aid Suluan on the 23rd, but still no transport was available. By the 27th they had assembled three Filipino-manned sailboats and 11 canoes and the 80 Rangers arrived on Suluan at 1100 hours on the 28th. The Japanese had again occupied the lighthouse. A direct assault was impossible on the narrow approach path, so Simons and 14 Rangers scaled the 300ft seaside cliff and surprised the enemy at 0200 hours. They killed 32 with the loss of one KIA and four WIA.

The Rangers conducted patrols on other Leyte Gulf islands into November killing a number of Japanese. In October Company C rounded up Japanese sailors from the sunken battleship *Yamashiro*. They also guarded Seabees constructing an airfield at Tanauan. The battalion was relieved by Leyte guerrillas and moved to Tolosa for Sixth Army HQ security on November 13. Company B on Suluan rejoined the battalion on the 14th.

The Luzon invasion and the Cabanatuan rescue
On January 1, 1945 the Rangers departed Tacloban with the Luzon invasion force (Operation MIKE I). The Sixth Army would land in Lingayen Gulf on northwest Luzon (SATANIC) on January 9 (S-Day) with four I and XIV Corps'

The Philippine guerrillas provided 106 two-wheel carabao carts like this to transport the sick and weakened liberated prisoners and 10 wounded Rangers from the Cabanatuan Prison Camp.

divisions. On S+1 the Rangers landed on Beach BLUE 2 in the I Corps sector following the 6th InfDiv, which had landed on S-Day. The battalion was assigned to secure the Sixth Army HQ at Dagupan, but also sent patrols into the hills. On the 15th a patrol reconnoitered Santiago Island on the northwest shoulder of the bay, but the Japanese had already evacuated.

On January 27 the battalion was alerted that it would stage a rescue operation for 500 American, British, and Dutch prisoners held at a camp near Cabanatuan (called Pangatian Camp in some documents; both names were nearby villages). The Sixth Army had advanced to within 40 miles of the camp as it drove south to Manila and it was feared the Japanese would murder or move the prisoners before the camp was reached. It was known through guerrillas that the prisoners were in poor physical condition. LtCol Mucci would lead the 128-man rescue force consisting of Company C (Capt Robert Price); 2d Platoon, Company F (1stLt Frank J. Murphy); two Alamo Scout teams (Nellist and Rounsaville Teams—14 men), and four men of Photo Unit F, 832d Signal Service Battalion; Filipino guerrillas would provide significant assistance. The Rangers departed from a guerrilla camp at Guimba at 1400 hours, January 28. There they left a radio team with an SCR-694 and carried one themselves to relay reports to higher headquarters. They borrowed additional bazookas from the 6th InfDiv as Japanese tanks were parked at the camp. While the Alamo Scouts placed the camp under surveillance, the 107 Rangers and 80 guerrillas under Capt Eduardo Joson marched 29 miles through enemy territory to link up with the Scouts, 90 more guerrillas, and 160 unarmed litter bearers under Capt Juan Pajota. Besides eluding the Japanese, there were also communist anti-American guerrillas of the People's Anti-Japanese Army (Hukbalahap) in the area that may have interfered with the operation. On the 29th the camp was reconnoitered further and a plan developed.

At 1945 hours, dusk, January 30 the Rangers attacked the camp, guarded by 73 Japanese with another 150 resting there on their way to the front. Another 800 were in Cabu 1 mile east. American aircraft strafed outside of the camp to distract the Japanese. As 1st Platoon, Company C (2dLt William J. O'Connell) attacked through the main gate to wipe out the guards and destroy parked tanks and trucks, 2d Platoon, Company F and the Alamo Scouts opened fire on guard posts at the camp's rear. They also doubled as a reserve. Company C's 2d Platoon (2dLt Melville Schmidt) followed the 1st Platoon through the gate to attack the transient unit and the guards' quarters. Sixty unarmed guerrillas then entered the camp to aid the freed prisoners. The Rangers killed 225 Japanese in 15 minutes, freed 513 prisoners, and began moving them back to friendly lines with the aid of guerrilla litter bearers.

The guerrillas established two roadblocks to delay Japanese reinforcements and covered the Rangers' withdrawal. Unknown to the Rangers the guerrillas had deployed another 400 men to back the roadblocks. More guerrillas with carabao carts and food met the force to help transport weakened prisoners. The column linked up with the 6th InfDiv at Sibual at 0800, 31st and the liberated prisoners were trucked to the 92d Evacuation Hospital. Two prisoners died of heart failure during the evacuation. Ranger losses were 10 WIA and two KIA, including Capt James C. Fisher, the battalion surgeon. The guerrillas fought exceptional rear guard actions without any losses, employing their four M1917A1 HMGs and two bazookas effectively enough to kill some 300 Japanese. In all the Japanese lost over 500 dead and 12 tanks destroyed. To this day the Cabanatuan raid is considered one of the classic Ranger operations in World War II, earning the participating units the Presidential Unit Citation.

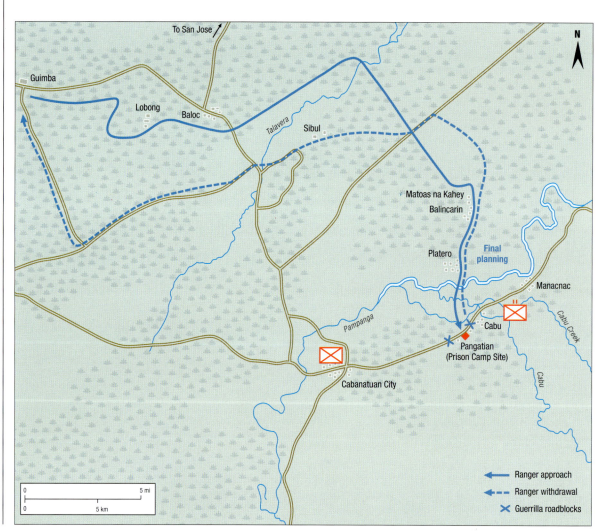

The Cabanatuan Prison Camp rescue, 6th Ranger Battalion, January 28–31, 1945.

The battalion continued to conduct company-size reconnaissance patrols and economy-of-force operations in the hills to check Japanese infiltration attempts into February. They interdicted and destroyed several of these attempts with minimal casualties. On February 10 the battalion was based at San Fernando, north of Manila. LtCol Mucci was reassigned as a regimental commander in the 6th InfDiv and promoted to colonel. The XO, Maj Garrett, took over, Capt Simons was assigned as the new XO, and both were promoted. (Mucci, Garrett, and Simons retired as colonels.) In April and May men with sufficient overseas time were rotated back to the States. Infantry replacements arriving at the replacement depot in Manila were asked if they desired to volunteer for the Rangers and were run through a Ranger course at San Fernando. Patrols in the area continued in support of the 6th InfDiv and the battalion provided Sixth Army HQ security.

At the end of May Company B was attached to the small Connolly Task Force formed by the 37th InfDiv. The task force departed on June 3 moving up Luzon's upper west coast and around the north end. Its mission was to prevent the enemy from escaping by that route as the rest of the 37th InfDiv pushed north on the island's east side. The task force secured the northeast coastal town of Aparri on June 21 and Camalaniugan Airfield to the south on the 23rd. Almost immediately, Gypsy Task Force (1/511 PIR), 11th AbnDiv parachuted on to the airfield.

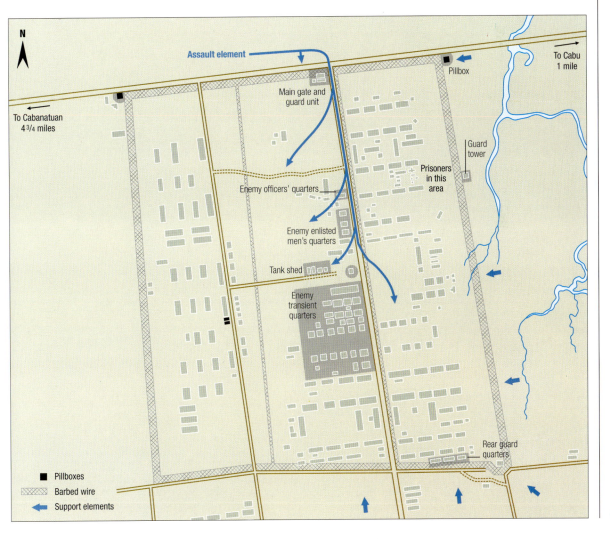

The raid on Cabanatuan Prison Camp, 1945 hours, January 30, 1945.

In July, 253 replacements arrived and by September 245 veterans had returned home. On September 15 the battalion arrived in Wakayama, Japan with the Sixth Army. It provided headquarters security and served as guards on trains transporting sensitive items. On December 30, 1945 it was inactivated at Camp Fisher (formerly Fushimi Barracks, renamed after the battalion surgeon who died at Cabanatuan) outside of Kyoto. Many Rangers were sent home; others, with short overseas time, were assigned elsewhere. The 6th Rangers was awarded the Philippine Presidential Unit Citation for its sterling service. In the event the war had continued, it was planned to transfer short-serving members of the 2d and 5th Rangers from Europe and train the 6th Rangers for the November 1945 invasion of Japan.

6th Ranger Battalion commanders		
Battalion CO	LtCol Henry A. Mucci	
	Maj Robert W. Garrett (LtCol 11 Jun 45)	10 Feb 45
	Maj Robert W. Price	Jul 45
Battalion XO	Maj Robert W. Garrett (acting CO 10–23 Oct 44)	
	Capt Arthur D. Simons (Maj 10 Jun 45)	10 Feb 45
	Capt Joe J. Shearon	July 45
HQ Company	1stLt James R. Berry	
	1stLt Clifford K. Smith	9 Oct 44
	Capt George F. Monsirratt	12 Nov 44
	Capt Leslie M. Gray	1 Aug 45
	1stLt John J. McCarthy	13 Sep 45
	2dLt J. A. Chaney	2 Oct 45
Company A	1stLt Nicholas F. Curi	
	Capt Norman J. Lever	12 Nov 44
	1stLt Robert Strandfeldt	30 Jul 45
Company B	Capt Arthur D. Simons	
	Capt Leo V. Strausbaugh	10 Feb 45
	1stLt Lawrence J. Evans	1 Aug 45
Company C	Capt Robert Price	
	1st Lt John J. Ditmars	10 Feb 45
	1stLt Joseph T. Poiesz	15 Apr 45
	1stLt Melville Schmidt	26 Jul 45
Company D	Capt Leslie M. Gray	
	Capt Tom J. Lyman	10 Feb 45
	2dLt Joseph T. Poiesz	25 Feb 45
	Capt Tom J. Lyman	15 Apr 45
Company E	1stLt Joe J. Shearon (Capt 1 Nov 44)	
	1stLt Joseph D. Mobley	30 Aug 45
Company F	1stLt Harold R. Jacobs (Capt Nov 44)	
	2dLt William F. Hume	25 Oct 45
Medical Det	Capt James C. Fisher	(KIA 30 Jan 45)
	1stLt Joseph T. Poiesz (acting)	30 Jan 45
	Capt Charles A. Parker	10 Feb 45

Lessons learned

While the value of the various Scout and Raider units was demonstrated in World War II, every single unit was deactivated by the end of 1945. While admittedly there was no pressing need for such units, the ability was lost to develop special units for projected future battlefields, integrate new weapons, equipment, and radios into these units, and refine their tactics and techniques. Another misfortune was the loss of extensive institutional knowledge possessed by the officers and men of special units. While many remained in the service it is not an easy task to assemble and reactivate special units. Former experienced special operators may be assembled, but it still requires a great deal of time to re-establish, train, adapt to the new situation and environment, and develop the units into effective organizations.

The Marine Corps was first to re-establish special units, in the form of amphibious reconnaissance units, in 1950. These eventually evolved into force reconnaissance companies. The Army organized airborne Ranger companies in 1950, but with no clear and realistic concept of employing them they were deactivated in 1951. Army Special Forces was organized in 1952, but it was not until 1961 that the Army rediscovered the value of long-range reconnaissance patrol companies along the lines of the Alamo Scouts. These eventually evolved into today's long-range surveillance units. Ranger battalions with a strike mission were not again organized until 1974 while the Marines have never re-established Raider units.

Many of the tactics, techniques, and procedures used by today's special operations forces are essentially the same or very similar to those used in World War II. Training methods (the Alamo Scouts' peer evaluation is used by the Rangers), scouting, patrolling, intelligence collection, and fieldcraft skills have changed little. Technology has changed some procedures such as communications (satellite radios), land navigation (Global Positioning System), and weapons employment (night-vision devices and sights). In the end though, it still requires highly motivated, physically fit, proficient, self-confident individuals working as a close-knit team of special men to accomplish special missions.

The remains of the Japanese Navy Kawanishi H8K2 "Emily" four-engine flying boat shot down by the 2d Raiders with machine guns and AT rifles. This still lay beached in the Makin lagoon when the 27th InfDiv seized the island 15 months later.

Chronology

1941
October 10 Scout Detachment (Prov) (Alaskan Scouts) formed.
December 7 Japan attacks Pearl Harbor.

1942
January Scout-Observer Group formed.
January 6 1st Separate Battalion activated.
January 23 2d Separate Battalion activated.
February 16 1st Separate Battalion redesignated 1st Raider Battalion.
February 19 2d Separate Battalion redesignated 2d Raider Battalion.
July 6 Allied Intelligence Bureau established by SWPA.
July 19 Combat Intelligence Unit reorganized as Intelligence Center/Pacific Ocean Area.
August 15 Amphibious Scout and Raider School established.
August 29 Prov Raider Battalion, 2d Marines formed.
September 20 3d Raider Battalion activated.
September 28 Prov Raider Battalion, 2d Marines disbanded.
October 23 4th Raider Battalion activated.

1943
January Prov Scout Battalion, 7th InfDiv formed.
January 7 Scout-Observer Group redesignated Amphibious Reconnaissance Company, Pacific Fleet.
March 15 1st Raider Regiment activated.
April 1 1st–4th Raider Battalions redesignated as units of 1st Raider Regiment.
May 24 Philippine Subsection, Section C, AIB reorganized as Philippine Regional Section.
June Prov Scout Battalion, 7th InfDiv disbanded.
July 1 978th Signal Service Company activated.
July 7 Special Service Unit No. 1 commissioned.
August 25 Amphibious Reconnaissance Company, Pacific Fleet redesignated VAC.
September 12 2d Raider Regiment (Prov) formed with 2d and 3d Raider Battalions.
November 6 Alaskan Scouts redesignated 1st Combat Intelligence Platoon.
5217th Reconnaissance Battalion (Prov) formed.
December 3 Alamo Scout Training Center established.

1944
January 1 Special Service Unit No. 1 redesignated Seventh Amphibious Force Scouts.
January 26 2d Raider Regiment (Prov) disbanded.
February 1 1st Raider Regiment deactivated and assets reorganized as 4th Marines (Separate).
April 14 Amphibious Reconnaissance Company, VAC reorganized and designated as battalion.
August 26 Amphibious Reconnaissance Battalion, VAC redesignated FMFPac.
September 24 6th Ranger Infantry Battalion activated.
November 20 5217th Reconnaissance Battalion (Prov) disbanded and assets activated as 1st Reconnaissance Battalion, Special.

1945

May 7	Germany surrenders (V-E Day).
August 6	Atomic bomb dropped on Hiroshima.
August 9	Atomic bomb dropped on Nagasaki.
August 14	Japan announces intent for unconditional surrender.
August 15	1st Reconnaissance Battalion, Special inactivated.
September	Amphibious Scout and Raider School decommissioned.
September 2	Japan surrenders (V-J Day).
September 24	Amphibious Reconnaissance Battalion, FMFPac deactivated.
November	Alamo Scouts disbanded.
December	Alaskan Scouts inactivated. Seventh Amphibious Force Scouts decommissioned.
December 30	6th Ranger Infantry Battalion inactivated.

Bibliography

Alexander, Joseph H. *Edson's Raiders: The 1st Marine Raider Battalion in World War II* (Annapolis, MD; Naval Institute Press; 2000)

Black, Robert W. *Rangers in World War II* (New York; Ballantine Books; 1992)

Breuer, William B. *The Great Raid on Cabanatuan: Rescuing the Doomed Ghosts of Bataan and Corregidor* (Hoboken, NJ; John Wiley & Sons Ltd; 1994)

Breuer, William B. *MacArthur's Undercover War: Spies, Saboteurs, Guerrillas, and Secret Missions* (Hoboken, NJ; John Wiley & Sons Ltd.; 1995)

Disette, Edward and Adamson, H. C. *Guerrilla Submarines* (New York; Ballantine Books; 1972)

Dwyer, John B. *Commandos from the Sea: The History of Amphibious Special Warfare in World War II and the Korean War* (Boulder, CO; Paladin Press; 1998)

Dwyer, John B. *Scouts and Raiders: The Navy's First Special Warfare Commandos* (Westport, CT; Praeger; 1993)

Garfield, Brian *The Thousand-Mile War: World War II in Alaska and the Aleutians* (New York; Doubleday; 1969)

Hoffman, Jon T. *From Makin to Bougainville: Marine Raiders in the Pacific War* (Washington, DC; Headquarters, Marine Corps; 1995)

Hoffman, Jon T. *Once a Legend: "Red Mike" Edson of the Marine Raiders* (Novato CA; Presidio Press; 1994)

Johnson, Forrest B. *Hour of Redemption: The Ranger Raid on Cabanatuan* (New York; Manor Books; 1978)

Love, Edmund G. *The Hourglass: A History of the 7th Infantry Division in World War II* (Nashville, TN; The Battery Press; 1988)

Meyers, Bruce F. *Swift, Silent, and Deadly: Marine Amphibious Reconnaissance in the Pacific, 1942–1945* (Annapolis, MD; Naval Institute Press; 2004)

Rosenquist, R.G.; Sexton, Martin Jr.; and Buerlein, Robert A. *Our Kind of War: Illustrated Saga of the U.S. Marine Raiders in World War II* (Richmond, VA; American Historical Foundation; 1990)

Rottman, Gordon L. *US Marine Corps Order of Battle: Ground and Air Units in the Pacific War, 1939–1940* (Westport, CT; Greenwood Publishing; 2001)

Rottman, Gordon L. *World War II Pacific Island Guide: A Geo-Military Study* (Westport, CT; Greenwood Publishing; 2001)

Sides, Hampton *Ghost Soldiers: The Epic Account of World War II's Greatest Rescue Mission* (New York; Anchor Books; 2002)

Smith, George W. *Carlson's Raid: The Daring Marine Assault on Makin* (Novoto, CA; Presidio Press; 2001)

Smith, Michael S. *Bloody Ridge: The Battle that Saved Guadalcanal* (New York; Pocket Books; 2000)

Stahl, Bob *You're No Good to Me Dead: Behind the Japanese Lines in the Philippines* [1st Reconnaissance Battalion] (Annapolis, MD; Naval Institute Press; 1995)

Stanton, Shelby L. *Order of Battle, U.S. Army, World War II* (Novato, CA; Presidio Press; 1984)

Stubbe, Ray W. *Arugha! The History of Specialized and Force-Level Reconnaissance Activities and Units of the United States Marine Corps, 1900–1974* (Washington, DC; Headquarters, Marine Corps; 1981)

Updegraph, Charles L., Jr. *U.S. Marine Corps Special Units of World War II* (Washington, DC; Headquarters, Marine Corps; 1972)

Zedric, Lance Q. *Silent Warriors of World War II: The Alamo Scouts Behind Japanese Lines* (New York; Pathfinder; 1995)

Abbreviations and linear measurements

AIB	Allied Intelligence Bureau	LVT	Landing Vehicle, Tracked ("amtrac")
Asst	Assistant	MarBde	Marine Brigade
ASTC	Alamo Scouts Training Center	MarDiv	Marine Division
AT	anti-tank	MIA	missing in action
BAR	Browning Automatic Rifle	NCO	non-commissioned officer
BCT	Battalion Combat Team (USA)	OSS	Office of Strategic Services
Bn	Battalion	Prov	Provisional
Co	Company	PRS	Philippine Regional Section
CO	Commanding Officer	SMG	submachine gun
CW	continuous wave (Morse Code radio transmission)	SSU #1	Special Service Unit No. 1
Det	Detachment	SWPA	Southwest Pacific Area
DOW	died of wounds	TF	Task Force
FLEX	Fleet Landing Exercise	TG	Task Group
FMF	Fleet Marine Force	TH	Territory of Hawaii
FMFPac	Fleet Marine Force, Pacific	T/O	Tables of Organization (USMC)
FSSF	First Special Service Force	T/O&E	Table of Organization and Equipment (USA)
GHQ	General Headquarters, SWPA		
HMG	heavy machine gun	UDT	Underwater Demolition Team
HQ	Headquarters	US	United States
HQMC	Headquarters, Marine Corps	USMC	United States Marine Corps
HQ&S	headquarters and service (company/battery)	USN	United States Navy
IIIAC	III Amphibious Corps	VAC	V Amphibious Corps
IMAC	I Marine Amphibious Corps	WIA	wounded in action
InfDiv	Infantry Division (US Army)	WO	Warrant Officer
JICPOA	Joint Intelligence Center/Pacific Ocean Area	XO	Executive Officer (second-in-command)
KIA	killed in action	(-)	less (elements detached from parent unit)
LMG	light machine gun	(+)	reinforced (additional elements attached)

Ship and landing craft classification codes

AGC	Amphibious Force Flagship
AKA	Attack Cargo Ship
APA	Attack Transport
APD	Fast Transport (aka destroyer-transport)
BB	Battleship
DD	Destroyer
DE	Destroyer Escort
LCI	Landing craft, infantry
LCP(R)	Landing craft, personnel (ramp)
LCR(L)/(S)	Landing craft, rubber (large)/(small)
LCVP	Landing craft, vehicle or personnel
LST	Landing ship, tank
PC	Submarine chaser
PT	Patrol torpedo boat
SS	Submarine

Officer Ranks

Marine and Army		**Navy**	
2dLt	2d Lieutenant	Ens	Ensign
1stLt	1st Lieutenant	Lt(jg)	Lieutenant (Junior Grade)
Capt	Captain	Lt	Lieutenant
Maj	Major	LCdr	Lieutenant Commander
LtCol	Lieutenant-Colonel	Cdr	Commander
Col	Colonel	Capt	Captain
BGen	Brigadier-General ("one-star")	Commo	Commodore
MajGen	Major-General ("two-star")	RAdm	Rear Admiral
LtGen	Lieutenant-General ("three-star")	VAdm	Vice Admiral

Distances, ranges, and dimensions are given in the contemporary US system of inches, feet, yards, and statute miles rather than metric:

feet to meters:	multiply feet by 0.3048
yards to meters:	multiply yards by 0.9144
miles to kilometers:	multiply miles by 1.6093

Index

Figures in **bold** refer to illustrations

1st Combat Intelligence Platoon 27
1st Parachute Battalion 54, 57, 72, **72**
1st Special Service Force 27
832d Signal Service Battalion 41, 85
978th Signal Service Company 41–2, 43
5217th/1st Reconnaissance Battalion 24
   casualties 43
   commanders 41
   insignia **39**
   organization 41, **41**, 42
   Philippines 39–40, **40**, 42–3
5218th Reconnaissance Company 41, 42

Advanced Intelligence Center 23
Alamo Scouts 10, 12, **14**, 17, 43–5, 89
   Bismarcks 45
   casualties 45
   commanders 44
   insignia **45**
   Japan 45
   Nellist Team **43**, 45, 85
   New Guinea 43–4, 45
   organization 43–4, 45
   Philippines **43**, 45, 85, 86
   Rounsaville Team 45, 85
Alamo Scouts Training Center 44, 45
Alaska National Guard 25
Alaskan Defense Command 25, 27, 75
Alaskan Scouts 12, 17
   Aleutian Islands **25**, 26–7, **27**
   casualties 27
   clothing 25–6, **26**, 27
   commanders 25, 26, 27
   insignia **28**
Alaskan Territorial Guard 25
Aleutian Islands 28
   Adak Island 26
   Amchitka Island **25**, 26, 27
   Attu Island **25**, 26–7, **27**, 59, 74, 75–9, **75**, 77–9
   Kiska Island **25**, 26, 27, 75
   Nunivak Island 27
   Unalaska Island 76
Allied Intelligence Bureau 23, 24, 39, 41, 42
Amphibious Corps
   Atlantic Fleet 28, 38, 49
   Pacific Fleet 28–9, 49, 65
Amphibious Force
   Atlantic Fleet 28
   Pacific Fleet 28
   South Pacific 62
Amphibious Reconnaissance Battalion
   commanders 32, 35
   insignia **28**
   Iwo Jima 34
   Japan/Home Islands 34–5
   Marianas 32–3, 34
   Marshalls 33
   Philippines 34
   organization 32, 33, **33**
Amphibious Reconnaissance Company
   casualties 30, 31
   commanders 28, 29, 30, 31

   Gilberts 29–30, **29**
   Marshalls 30–1
   organization 28, **32**
Amphibious Scout and Raider School 38–9
Amphibious Scout School 35, 39
Amphibious Scouts 12, 17, 39
   commanders 37, 38
   insignia **37**
   New Britain 37
   New Guinea 37
   SSU No. 1 **35–6**, 37, 38, 43, 44, **82**, 83
   tactics/techniques 37
   Third Amphibious Force 35
Amphibious Training Bases 38
Amphibious Training Staff 28
Army Language School 41
AT rifles 17, 19, 51, 54, **58–9**, 60, **60–1**, **66**, 82, 89
attack transports 30, 31, 32, 34, 35
Australia 6, 23, 35, 37, 41, 44, 80
Australian New Guinea Police Force 35, 37

barges/longboats 10, 27
BARs 16, 17, 18, 28, 32, **32–3**, **44**, 47, **49**, 51, 54, **54**, **56**, **58–9**, 61, 61, 65, 76, 80, 81
bazookas 15, 17, 19, **19**, 32, **33**, **66**, 81, 85
Beach Party Training Camp 38
beacon/signal lights 39, **82**, 83, 84
Beans, LtCol Fred **20**
binoculars/telescopes **22**, 27
Bismarck Islands 23, 24, 37, 45
boats 7, 13, **14**, 26, 27, 28, 30, 37, 42, 45, 84
Buretoni Mission Trail 72

Cabanatuan Prison Camp **43**, 45, **84**, 85–7, **85–7**
Canangra Jungle Warfare School 41
canoes/kayaks 7, 14, 28, 42, 84
carabao carts 42, **85**, 86
carbines **9**, 16, 17, 18, **18**, 27, 28, 32, **32–3**, 37, 43, **43–4**, 47, 51, **56**, **58**, **61**, 65, 76, 80, 82
cargo ships 51, 53
Carlson, LtCol Evans F. 46, 49, 53, **53**, 59, 60, **60**, 61, **61**, 65
Central Philippines Attack Force 83
Coastwatchers 6, 23, 24, 25, 41, 62, 68
Combat Intelligence Platoon 12
Combat Intelligence Unit 23
Commandos 6, 12, 44, 46, 48, 49, 53, 81
Communist guerrillas 85
Connolly Task Force 87
Consolidated PBY Catalina 8, **8**, **69**
Counter-Intelligence Corps 43

demolition charges **6**
destroyer escorts 47, 65, **65**
destroyer-transports 7, 11, 12, 13, 15, 31, 32, 34, **35**, 47, **47**, 48, 50–1, 52, **52**, 53, 65, **65**, 77, 83, 84
destroyers 13, 30, 42, 52, 83
Dinagat Attack Group 83
dog sleds 26, 27
Distinguished Unit Citation 79

Eastern Landing Force 68, **70**
Eastern Landing Group 33

Edson, LtCol Merritt A. **20**, 48, 49, 50, 51, 53, 56–7, 65
Engineer Amphibious Command 35, **37**
Eniwetok Expeditionary Group 31
"Eskimo Scouts" 25
Espíritu Santo 61, 62, 63, 64, 69

Fifth Amphibious Force 35
Fiji Guerrillas 23
flags/marker panels 22, 39
flamethrowers 65, 82
FLEX 4/6/7 28, 47
flying boats 7, 8, **8**, 13, **14**, 19, 30, 45, 60, **69**, 89
Fourth Army Replacement Depot 76

GHQ/SWPA 23, 24, 39, 42–3
Gilbert Islands
   Apamama Atoll 29–30, **29**, 31
   Kotabu Island 30
   Little Makin Island 59
   Makin Atoll/Island 15, 19, 29, 30, **53**, **57**, 59–61, **60**, 62, **62**, 89
Goss, Marine Gunner Angus H. **6**
grenade launchers 16, 17, **56**, 82
grenades 16, 18, **18**, 61, 76, **84**
Gypsy Task Force 87

Islands Coastwatching Service 24
Iwo Jima 34

Japan/Home Islands 43, 88
   Hokkaido 59
   Kyushu 45
   Okinawa 34–5
JIC/POA 23
Joint Alaskan Staff 75
Jones, Maj James L. 28, 29, 30, 31, 32, 35

Kawanishi H8K2 "Emily" 19, 60, **89**
knives/machetes 18, 27, 32, 43, 82
Korea 39
Krueger, LtGen Walter 43, 45, 80, 83
Kume Shima Landing Force **33**

landing craft **4**, 7, **10**, 14, 15, 26, **27**, 31, 35, **35**, 38, 39, 45, 52, 62, 77, 84
life rafts **9**, 19, 28
litter bearers 85, 86
Liversedge, Col Harry B. 63, 64–5, 72
Luzon Invasion Force 84–5

"M" Force 41
MacArthur, Gen Douglas 23, 35, 42, 80
machine guns 15, 16, 17, 18, 28, 32, **32–3**, **39**, 51, 54, **58–9**, 60, **60–1**, 65, **66**, 76, 79, 81, 89
Majuro Attack Group 31
Mariana Islands
   Saipan 32–3, 34
   Tinian 34, 59
Marshall Islands
   Arno Atoll 31
   Engebi Island 31
   Eniwetok Atoll 31
   Kwajalein Atoll 31, 61
   Majuro Atoll 30–1

95

Parry Island 31
Saipan 33, 34
Medal of Honor 57, 60
Meritorious Unit Citation 43
Mobile Landing Group 47
Morse Code 8, 10, 20–1, 22, 25, 39, 41, 45
mortars 15, 17, 18–19, **18**, 30, 32, **32–3**, 51, 54, **58–61**, 65, **66**, 76, 79, 80, 81
Mucci, Col Henry A. 80, 81, **81**, 85, 87
mules 80, 81

Native Americans 10, 25, 53
native guides/porters 23, **23–4**, 30, 35, 37, 60, 61, 62, **69**
Navajo code talkers 10, 53
Naval Combat Demolition Units 38
Naval Group, China 38, 39
Naval Intelligence 35
Navy Unit Commendation 35, 57
Netherlands East Indies Intelligence Service 23
Netherlands New Guinea 37, 38, 42, 43, **44**, 45
New Britain 43
    Arawe 37
    Cape Gloucester 37
    Gasmata 37
    Piva Trail 72, **74**
New Caledonia 54, 57, 63, 69
New Georgia 17, 63, 64, **64**, 68–9, **68**
    Bairoko Harbor 69, **69**
    Dragons Peninsula 69, **71**
    Enogai Inlet 69, **69**
    Gatukai Island 69
    Lambeti 68
    Munda Point 68, 69
    Regi Plantation 15, 68
    Rendova Island 68
    Segi Point 15, 68, **70**
    Vanguru Island 68
    Viru Harbor **67**, 68
    Wickham Anchorage 68, **70**
New Guinea 23, 24, 35, **36**, **43–4**, 69, **69**, 71, **71**, 80
    Fergusson Island 37, 44, 45
    Finschhafen 37, 45, 81
    Tananmerah Bay 83
New Hebrides 61, 62, 63, 64, 69
Northern Landing Force 76, 77, 79, **79**
Northern Landing Group 69, **71**

Pacific Ocean Area **5**, 35
Pearl Harbor 23, 29, 48, 52, 57, **57**, 61
People's Anti-Japanese Army 85
Philippine Presidential Unit Citation 43, 88
Philippine Regional Section
    casualties 42
    commanders 39, 40, 41, 42
    guerrilla contact 39, **39**, 42–3
    Kopp/Philips Parties 42
    "Mission Men" 41, 43
    Netherlands New Guinea 42
    Parachute Section 42
    Philippines 39–40, 42–3
Philippine Subsection 39
Philippines 15, 23, 24, 35, **40**, 80
    Dinagat Island **82**, 83, 84
    guerrillas 30, 39, **39**, 42–3, 84, **85**, **85**, 86
    Guimba 85
    Homonhon Island 83, 84
    Leyte 38, 39, 42, 43, 45, 82–4, **82–3**
    Leyte Gulf 82, **82–3**, 84
    Luzon 39–40, 43, **43**, 45, 84–8, **84–7**

Mindoto 42
Morotai Island 37, 42
Sabual 86
Sulan Island 83–4
Tacloban 84
Tolosa 84
Philippines Civil Affairs Unit 43
pistols 16, 17, 27, 37, 43, **43–4**, **58**, **61**, **66**, 80, 81, **81**, 82
Presidential Unit Citation 86
Provisional Scout Battalion 17, 18
    7th InfDiv 74–9, **75**, **77–9**
    7th Reconnaissance Troop 76, 77, 78, 79
    7th Scout Company 76, 77–8, 79
    Attu Island 74, 75–9, **75**, **77–9**
    casualties 78, 79
    commanders 76, 77, 78, 79
    insignia **74**
    organization **74**, 76

radios **6**, 7, 8, 10, 14, 20–2, **21**, 24, 28, 39, 45, 53, 76, 79, 85
Raider Battalions 4, **7**, 20, 21, **21**, **23**, 24, 38
    1st **6**, 9, **20**, **47**, 50–4, **50**, **53**, 57, **58–9**, **61**, 63, **68**, 69
    1st (Separate) **20**, 48, 49
    2d **18**, **24**, **49–50**, 53–4, **54**, 57, **57**, 59–62, **59–62**, 63, **63**, 65, 69, 71–2, **89**
    2d (Separate) 49, **53**
    3d **20**, 53, **60–1**, 63–4, 69, 72, **72**
    4th 53, **54**, **60–1**, 64, **65**, **67**, 68–9, **68**, **70**
    casualties 54, 57, 60, 61, 62, 68, 69, **69**, 72, 73
    commanders 46, 48, 49, 50, 51, 53, **53–4**, 57, 59, 60, **60**, 61, **61**, 63, 64–5, 69, 72, 73
    commendations 57
    Gilberts 15, 19, **53**, **57**, 59–61, **60**, **62**, **89**
    insignia **48**
    "Long Patrol" **24**, **53**, **61**, 62, **63**
    New Caledonia 69
    New Georgia 15, 17, **67**, 68–9, **68–71**
    New Hebrides 61, 62, 63, 64, 69
    organization **6**, 11, 12, **47**, 49, **49**, 50–4, **54**, 56, **56**, **58–9**, 60, **60**, 61, **61**, 64, 65, **65**, **68**, 69
    Russell Islands 63–4, **66**
    Solomons **6**, 17, **18**, **24**, **48–51**, 53, 54, 56–7, **58–9**, 61, 63, **63**, 68, 69, 71–2
    tactics/techniques **6**, 6, 7, 8, 9–10, **10**, **46**, 50
    training 7, 8–10, **8–10**, **13**, **46**, 50, 61, 68
    weapons **6**, 16, 17, **17**, 18, **18**, 19, **46**, 47, **49**, 51, 53, 54, **54**, 56, **58–9**, 60, **60**, 61, **61**, 65, **66**
Raider-Parachute Battalion 54, **55**, 56–7
Raider Regiments 53
    1st 12, **61**, 64–5, 66, **66**, 69, 72, 73
    2d 69, 72
Raider Replacement Training Battalion **8**
Raider Replacement Training Company 64, 66
Raider Training Battalion 66, 72
Rangers 11–12, 21–2, 44, 46, 48, 52, 53, **80**, 89
    1st Ranger Battalion 81
    2d Ranger Battalion 88
    5th Ranger Battalion 88
    6th Ranger Battalion 9, 22, 45, 80–8
    casualties 84, **85**, 86, 87
    commanders 84, 85, 86, 87, 88
    insignia **82**
    organization 6, 80, 81, **82**
    Philippines 15, 82–8, **82–7**
    weapons 17, 18, 80, 81–2, **81–2**, **84**, 86
Reconnaissance Battalion, Special 11
Regimental Landing Group 17 76

rifles 16, 17, **17**, 18, **18**, 26, 27, 28, 32, **32–3**, **43–4**, 47, **49**, 51, 54, **54**, **56**, **58**, 61, **61**, **66**, 76, 79, 80, 81, 82
Roosevelt, LtCol James 46, 49, **54**, 60, 64, 65
rubber boats 7, 8, **9**, 10, 13, **13**, 14, 15, 19, **19**, 20, 26, 28, 30, 31, 34, **35**, 37, 39, 44, 45, 46, **46**, 47, 50, 59, 60, 61, **65**, 68, 76, 77, 81
Russell Islands **17**, 63–4, **66**

Scout and Raider School 44
Scout-Observer Group 28, 38
scout-observers 4, 6, **6**, 20, 21, 22, **22–3**, 24
Scouts 4, 6, **6**, 7, 8, **8**, 9–10, **9–10**, 11, **14**, 16, **17**, 18, 19, **19**, 20–2, **21**, 30, 38, 52
Sea Warfare School 41
Seventh Amphibious Force 35, 37, 38
Seventh Amphibious Force Scouts 37–8, 39
Seventh Fleet 35, 39
shotguns **44**, **59**, **66**
Signal Corps Training Center 41
Silverthorn Jr, Capt Merwin H. 28, 29, 31, 32
Sixth Army 43, 44, 45, 80, 84, 85, 87, 88
skis/snowshoes 26, **26**, 27
Smith, MajGen Holland 46, 47
sniper rifles 17, **17**, 51, 53, **58–9**, **61**, 80
Solomon Islands 14, 23, **23**, 24, 48
    Bougainville **18**, **20**, 69, 71–2, **72**
    Florida Island **50**
    Guadalcanal 17, **20**, **24**, **49–50**, 53, **53**, 54, 56–7, **58**, **59**, **59**, 61–2, **61**, 63, **63**, 68, 69, 72, 76, 80
    Koiari Beach 72, **72**
    Savo Island 56
    Torokina Island **20**
    Tulagi Island **6**, **51**, 54, 59
Southern Landing Force 76, 78–9
Special Forces Qualification Tab 45
Station KAZ 41, 42, 43
submachine guns 16, **16**, 17, **17**, 18, 27, 32, 43, **43–4**, **46**, 47, **49**, 51, 54, **54**, **56**, **58–9**, 65, **66**, 76, 80, 81, 82
submarines 7, 11, 14, **14**, 15, 19, 20, 22, 26, 28, 29, 30, 37, 39, 41, 42, 43, 45, **47**, **57**, 59, 60, 76, 77
surgeons 51, 53, 86

tally machines 24
tractors/trucks/vehicles 4, **27**, 31, 34, 51, 52, 53, 65, 66, 72, 82, 86
Turnage, MajGen Allen **20**

UDTs 34, 38, 52
US Army
    X/XIV/XXIV Corps 34, 38, 39, 68, 84–5
    infantry units 25, 26, **27**, 28, 29, 30, 31, 34, 35, 37, 40–1, 42, 43, 61–2, 63, 64, 68, 69, 71, 72, 74–9, **75**, **77–9**, 83, 84, 85, 86, 87, **89**
US Marine Corps
    brigades 28, 63, 73
    divisions **20**, 28, 29, 31, 34, 35, 37, 47, 48, 49, 54, 56, 62, 65, 69, 71–2, 73
    regiments **20**, 28, 29, 30, 31, 33, 46, 47, 48, 54, 56, 57, 62, 63, 71, 72, 73

"walkie-talkies" **6**, 21, **21**
Western Landing Force 68
Western Signal Corps Training Center 41
Whitney Sr, Col Courtney 39, 40, 41, 42

"Z" Force 41